Falling Out *of the* *Boat*

Maureen McCauley

The events and conversations in this book have been set down to the best of the author's recollection, although some names and details may have been changed to protect the privacy of individuals.

Printed in the United States of America.

Print ISBN: 978-1-09832-802-3
eBook ISBN: 978-1-09832-803-0

For my father, and in loving memory of my mother

*If there is a fear of falling, the only safety
consists in deliberately jumping.*

— Carl Jung

Do you wish to rise? Begin by descending.

— Saint Augustine

*Remain true to yourself, but move
ever upward
toward greater consciousness and
greater love...
For everything that rises must converge.*

— Teilhard de Chardin

Contents

	Prologue	
1	Red Rover	5
2	Exile	7
3	Run	14
4	First Steps	17
5	Boat Ballet	20
6	Initiation	23
7	Paradise Lost	27
8	Floating	33
9	Sculling School	37
10	Slip Slidin'	41
11	Sculling	46
12	Opacity	51
13	Spitfire Training	55
14	Inexorability	60
15	Women's Four	65
16	Fear Versus Desire	71
17	Head of the Charles	74
18	Falling Out of the Boat	80
19	Roaming	85
20	Bow	91
21	Seceding	95
22	Leaving	102
23	Competing	106
24	Return to Sculling School	109
25	Tempest	115
26	Rowing to Eden	121
27	Disobedience	128
28	Truth	136
	Epilogue	145
	Acknowledgments	148

Prologue

The first time I saw a scull, it was bobbing upside down on a swollen choppy river. It was the Ides of March. The sky had a slate tinge that warned of snow. There was a black-greenish cast to the river as though the violent departure of winter ice had bruised the water as it left. The scull rose and fell as each wave hit.

I was in an eight-person rowing shell and the boat's coxswain, after watching the sculler repeatedly try but fail to get back into the boat, relayed commands for us to row over and rescue him. It seemed preposterous to me that something the width of a pencil and length of a stretch limo could even be a boat. I couldn't imagine at the time what would possess someone to do something as certifiable as sculling. I knew I'd never do anything that crazy.

A scull is the longest, skinniest carbon-fiber shark on the water. Twenty-six feet long and twelve inches wide, the boat is designed for one purpose: slicing through water. Its beauty is the same as a samurai blade: intent. Moving powerfully, effortlessly, gracefully, a scull evinces its true nature.

Sculls are tippy, balance is not a given. Because the natural configuration of a scull is upside down, an oar on each side is essential for equilibrium in this high-wire act. The algebra of sculling demands that what one nine-foot oar does on the right side of the boat must be duplicated exactly on the left side.

In the muscle-powered small craft league, a canoe or kayak is a sensible choice for going out on rivers and lakes: you can see where you're going and the odds favor staying dry. Even though these boats can also capsize, it takes more than a momentary lapse of attention.

So how did I, someone who tried to always act sensibly, think rationally, save for a rainy day, and practice moderation in all things, end up on a river in a long, tippy spear of a boat?

I was asked that question one summer morning, by a man fishing on the dock I had just pulled alongside of in my scull.

"Pourquoi?" he inquired. Why?

I noticed Canada's red maple leaf on his tackle box and hoped I could remember enough college French to answer his question. I wondered if he had the same idea about preposterousness and craziness that I had when I first saw a scull. My answer, "because it connects me body and soul to the universe," seemed impossible to convey given language limitations, so I retreated to playing charades and pointed in the general direction of my waist, which he translated as *mange*, eat.

I shook my head and pointed to my heart.

"Ah, coeur!" Heart.

Then I recalled the word I was looking for, *ame*, soul. *"Coeur et ame?"* he asked. Heart and soul?

I nodded and added *"corps et ame."* Body and soul.

I scull because it connects me body and soul to the rhythm of the universe.

"Going to Sunday School" was a game I dreamed up and loved to play as a child. It required a wading pool, a sibling, and imagination. My sister and I, in our ruffle-bottomed bathing suits, would hold hands, pretend we were dressed in our Sunday best, and while singing "We're going to Sunday school, we're going to Sunday school," walk toward the pool until our bare feet made contact with its yellow plastic bumper. Then we'd jump into the water. Scripted distress followed: "We've ruined our dresses, what are we going to tell mother?" We'd splash around a bit, get out, and do it again and again.

The game was about dutifully setting out to do what was expected, marching down the path of propriety and falling Alice in Wonderland-like into a hole in the universe that took us to an unexpected place. I loved the surprise of finding myself in cool water instead of church, an unanticipatedly refreshing salvation.

As I was to learn, a scull is a carapace, too light to offer the protection of rationality, which is seldom the path the heart follows to love. A scull does, however, offer transport to solitude, connection of body and soul, and sometimes, transcendence. It also ferries accidental explorers to unintended discovery.

I did everything wrong. Sculling requires ease around water, I had none. What I thought was going to happen--sculling would be the same as rowing minus seven other people, ballet minus bloody toes--didn't. Instead, I had experiences I didn't expect and never sought, and those experiences changed me. Sculling baptized me into a new life, a life with moments of grace and sweet harmony. Slowly, inexorably, one stroke at a time, water was my teacher.

This is a story about discovery and an explorer guided by a carbon-fiber Virgil. The explorer, though not the least bit intrepid, is determined, which sometimes works just as well.

1
Red Rover

"Red Rover, Red Rover, we call Maureen over."

I am called. Hands gripping mine unclasp. I step back, then launch into a run, arms pumping, legs churning. I run so fast and hard that I fear for a second I will stumble and fall. "Faster, faster," I hear in my head. I am purpose. Then my stride lengthens and I am all smooth cheetah motion. Time slows to an easy, forever lope. It feels as if I am gliding on a current of air. The impact of braced arms on my chest surprises me. Momentarily, immovable and irresistible forces balance, but my momentum upsets that equilibrium. Hands open, outstretched arms drop. I am through the line.

I was the Red Rover Queen of Yeadon, P.A. Last called to challenge, never captured. A javelin whistling through air.

I was seven years old that summer. Skinny Minnie Fishtail was my father's nickname for me. He sang the name off-key, the entire lyric consisting of nothing but "Skinny Minnie Fishtail." I loved my father's song, and I loved having a special name. A different name. Maureen, attentive to expectations, did everything asked of her, could even eat an ice cream cone on a hot summer day without dripping any on her starched dress. A good girl because her mother told her she only loved good girls. Skinny Minnie Fishtail, though, could streak to home base untagged, climb to the top of monkey bars, and break through a Red Rover line. Skinny Minnie Fishtail was fearless, fierce, fast. Did my father give me the name because he saw something in me that summer, something that hadn't been there before? Did he see Skinny Minnie Fishtail long before I did?

Running toward that Red Rover line, I concentrated on finding the rhythm that would carry me to a dream current where I lost awareness of everything but the sense that I was floating, gliding. I felt whole there, connected body and soul. When I ran, my legs beat a rhythm my body and mind danced to. I raced until my heart pounded. Then I listened to the *thumpa thumpa* beat, the sound of me.

I ran in disobedience. "Don't run," my mother warned as I set off at a sprint to somewhere. Running was dangerous. I could fall and hurt myself. I wanted to be a good girl, to obey my mother, but there was a rightness about running that made its sacrifice to allay her fears seem wrong.

Looking through memory's pane, I see that my father was right about my name. I was meant to have a fishtail, a sleek silvery fan for floating on a dream current. As I replay the image of me running toward that Red Rover line, joy in every stride, I want to shout a warning to Skinny Minnie Fishtail: *Keep running. Run for your life. Don't stop.*

2
Exile

That summer, I'd leave the house early in the morning when dew was still on the grass and tour the neighborhood, sniffing for something that interested me: a tar bubble to burst, hollyhocks to fashion into dolls, creek water and dirt to mix until I got the batter thick enough to bake on sunny rocks. I plucked nectar-coated strands from inside white-and-yellow honeysuckle blossoms and rolled them over my tongue, pretending I was a bear. I was water finding a channel.

In early evening, I'd gather with about twelve other children from the neighborhood in the middle of our dead-end street. We'd play dodgeball, softball, hide-and seek, whatever was shouted out first in answer to "What d'ya wanna do?" We played until the first flickers from lightning bugs signaled the approach of night, and calls from front porches summoning us home began.

I never thought those days of wandering and exploring and evenings of running with the full flight of my being would end, but time turned a corner after that summer. As families of the neighborhood children I had played games with moved to the suburbs, choruses of "Red Rover, Red Rover" no longer resounded on the block.

My family joined our migrating Yeadon neighbors and moved to an area of rolling hills about twenty miles from Valley Forge. It was a lovely place to live, but the road in front of the house was a thoroughfare, not a place to play Red Rover or Monkey in the Middle. There were no sidewalks on which to roller skate or even play hopscotch. The few children my age who lived there mostly stayed indoors, where they sat in recreation rooms watching television.

I stopped running, playing tag, climbing monkey bars. I tried roller-skating in our driveway but the surface was too rough for continuous movement; when my wheels seized, I lost my balance and fell on to the macadam, bloodying my hands and knees. In Yeadon, I had jumped rope during recess with the girls in my class, but the girls at my new parochial school preferred standing in small groups talking about which boys liked them. I started to feel heavy, slow, thick—gravity's child now, not the Red Rover Queen of Yeadon, P.A. The Skinny Minnie Fishtail voice urging me to run *faster, harder* fell silent. I lost my way to the place where time and motion converged, where I was fearless.

As I fell deeper into inertia, I tried to catch hold of something that might halt my descent. If nearby ponds froze in deep winter, I ice skated after school, but just for a week or two until temperatures crept upward, melting the ice. Eventually, bereft of opportunities for focused rhythmic movement, my bridge to a world of timelessness and dreams, a place I once loved to go, disappeared.

Occasionally, I was reminded of my past. The summer before I started high school, my parents decided that typing would be a useful skill for me to learn. I was enrolled in a typing course offered by the local public high school as part of its summer school program. A tennis course was added to my summer curriculum to give my mother some chauffeuring relief by extending the time between school drop-off and pick-up.

The tennis courts were behind the school, fenced islands in the middle of hockey and lacrosse fields. The green concrete courts, brighter than the surrounding grass and smooth as licked ice cream, shimmered in the summer sun. Although instruction began in the heat of the day, it didn't matter to me how hard the sun beat down. Nothing mattered except that I was running, moving, concentrating on hitting the ball. When tennis ended, I went back to my sedentary world. But during those eight weeks of summer school, I had been a body set in motion.

After my tennis class, I anticipated that starting high school there would mean a return to a more active life, one in which I whacked balls across a net as part of physical education classes. But I didn't go to that school. Instead, under protest, I went to a Catholic high school, one in which boys and girls attended classes in separate wings of a Pentagon-sized building. A no-man's land that couldn't be crossed without properly authorized documents divided the wings.

During my first gym class, I saw equipment parked along the walls: balance beams, balls of various dimensions, nets attached to metal standards. I hoped that it was there to be used for some physical activity but it rarely was. Classes mostly consisted of inspection of our pleated, maize-colored, knee-length uniforms for conformity with standards of modesty and identification, followed by standing around until the bell rang for change of classes. The instructor made notes on her clipboard about the condition of each girl's uniform.

"Sew your name and homeroom number on the front before the next class. Do you hear me?"

"Put some starch in that uniform and don't roll it up in a ball in your locker. Do we understand each other?"

"I am not blind, unhike those skirts."

My grade, a B or maybe even an A, was based on my ironing and cross-stitching skills.

I thought standing-around-doing-nothing gym classes were behind me when I started college. Archery, badminton, square dancing, swimming, golf were just a few of the courses offered as part of the physical education smorgasbord. There were also tennis courts across from every dorm complex and a women's physical education building with a pool, squash courts, dance studio, rifle range, and fencing room. I thought I had found the athletic Promised Land. What I didn't know was that the faculty of the women's physical education department was fighting a war for academic respect, and everyone, including the students, was deemed the enemy. Determined to demonstrate that volleyball had the same level of difficulty as chemistry or physics, these instructors gave failing or near-failing grades routinely: D's and F's that counted toward your cumulative average because pass/fail wasn't an option then. After hearing dorm stories about 4.0s ruined by D's in bowling, I resolved to avoid that fate.

I signed up for tennis as my first class. I practiced on the courts across from my dorm and won all my matches. I knew how to score and had studied the rule book. I didn't think the written final would be a problem. I was hoping for an A.

The final, administered on the tennis court, required calculating angles of incidence, or maybe it was cosines. I remember it now as questions about trains leaving stations in Chicago and Pittsburgh and heading toward one another on the same track, except that tennis balls were involved. With an A for my match wins and a curved D for the final, I ended up with a C.

I took badminton, fencing, volleyball, and square dancing with the understanding that the instructor viewed any success on my part as failure on hers. I resigned myself to inevitable C's, acquired the credits I needed, and failed volleyball.

Ice skating, my last class, was taught by an adjunct instructor who had skated competitively. I spent the first week learning how to fall. The principle was simple: don't resist when you feel yourself headed for the ice. Rather than trying to break a fall with small-boned, easily snapped body parts, present your largest, most cushioned muscle to the ice as you go down.

By the end of that first week, my largest and most cushioned muscle was sore and bruised, but I had lost my fear of falling on the ice. I could risk. I accepted the possibility of failure inherent in attempting to balance on a blade the width of a knife edge. I learned that failure was part of learning, not its terminus. At the time, I thought I was learning how to ice skate, just as years afterward I'd learn about fear, loss, grace, forgiveness, balance, all while I thought I was learning how to scull.

Because anticipating and preventing falling didn't consume all my time on the ice, I could concentrate on feeling for an inside or outside edge, the flat of my blade. I listened for the sound of a clean stroke. I glided in silence, in a world of my own making, the rhythm of my blades stroking the ice becoming rhythm in my head. I spun, delighted by the slight effort it took. On one leg, the other raised behind me in arabesque, I floated around the rink.

The final was a two-minute routine, self-choreographed. I figure-eighted and arabesqued and spiraled and spun. I threw in a couple of T-stops that shaved ice fine enough for margaritas. I went through my planned program in thirty seconds, and after that, I made it up. That was the part I remember as 24-karat joy.

Married right after graduation, I followed my second lieutenant husband to different army bases and duty stations for three years. As expectation demanded, I packed away tennis racket and ice skates to pursue the grail of domestic bliss. But I found myself inventing reasons for walking almost anywhere instead of driving. At the time, I didn't question why I walked on the shoulders of busy roads or on sidewalks slammed by the noise of cars and trucks speeding by. I could not see the desperation that put me on those paths. All I knew was that no matter how noisy and unpleasant it was, I felt more alive moving.

Decades afterward, I read about "flow," a state of complete and focused involvement in an activity. Mihály Csíkszentmihályi, who researched the phenomenon, found that during flow, "the ego falls away. Time flies. Every action, movement and thought follows inevitably from the previous one, like playing jazz. Your whole being is involved..."

When I read Csíkszentmihályi's definition of flow, I replayed an image of Skinny Minnie Fishtail running toward a Red Rover line in my mind and remembered that time did fly; my whole being was involved. If those researchers had wired my seven-year-old skull to measure my brain waves, I was certain they would have concluded that what I had experienced was flow.

Although it was interesting to know that the joy I had felt in heart, mind, body, and soul was real, somehow I had always sensed that. What I did not know and couldn't imagine at the time was that the voice inside me, urging me to run faster and harder, was inextinguishable.

I was under a spell, a conviction that what had been lost was gone forever. As with all deep spells, there was a way to break this one, but not by tried-and-true methods such as knitting nettle coats or concocting potions under a full moon. Instead, awakening would require eyes on the past while moving forward in a spear of a boat.

3

Run

I was in law school when I came across a picture of seven-year-old me taken that Red Rover summer that gripped me with bony-handed truth. The photograph was in my baby book, given to me by my mother when I turned twenty-five, along with report cards and clippings she had saved from a local newspaper that informed the community I was an essay contest winner, an Honor Society inductee, a Dean's List student.

I was miserable. I spent my days sitting in amphitheater classrooms wondering why I ever thought law school would be an intellectual experience. I spent my nights trying to figure out what a holder in due course was. Sometimes I read Tolstoy or P.J. Wodehouse for survival.

Good grades and high test scores had gotten me to this place. A lifetime of silencing intuition, blindfolding instinct, and burying desire in the graveyard of duty kept me there. I hated myself for staying, even though it was the sensible and rational thing to do given my dismal job prospects as an English major. I was as lost as Dante in his dark wood.

I had come to this city in upstate New York, where winter and much of spring consisted of endless days of dispiriting grayness, because after my husband's discharge from the Army, we had decided to attend graduate school at the same time. That decision limited us to this one place in the United States that had both a Ph.D. program in criminal justice and an American Bar Association-accredited law school.

There was something in that blonde child's clear-eyed gaze that made me think she would be living a life different from mine, that she knew something important I had forgotten, and if I studied the photograph, I would know too. I'd look at the picture of her and then look in the mirror. No resemblance. She was lit from within; I looked sad, resigned. I found more pictures of her: posing in a satin mouse costume during a back-yard circus, running into the ocean, standing astride her two-wheeler. I loved her promise, but she was a ghost. I wondered what she'd tell me if I could talk to her. Would she know how to direct me back to the path I had lost?

Nietzsche said that if you stare into an abyss long enough, the abyss will stare back at you. He didn't say anything about someone talking to you from the abyss, but I have no other explanation for what happened.

It was late, around midnight. I had been studying for a commercial law exam and still had hours of reading ahead of me. I was in the haze of the Uniform Commercial Code when I heard:

Run.

I heard it so clearly and undeniably, I began to argue.

"Now? It's midnight. What about my test?"

Run.

I knew it was crazy to think I heard a command to run. I was alone in the room.

Run.

"You've got to be kidding!"

Run.

I knew somehow that I should not, could not, disobey that voice. I put on my clearance-sale sneakers and ran to the end of my block and then back home. I estimated that I had run a tenth of a mile. I felt as though a switch had been thrown somewhere inside me.

4
First Steps

I continued running my sidewalk loop late at night. I liked having the night to myself. When winter arrived, and with it snow-covered, icy sidewalks, I followed the city natives' practice of retreating indoors until spring, but missed my nocturnal run. This time, instead of returning to my slug-like existence, I looked for an indoor activity to substitute for running.

I couldn't find a Red Rover league, but I did learn of an adult ballet class for which no prior dance experience was required. I loved watching Sugar Plum dance in "The Nutcracker." She looked so graceful, so ethereal, and there was all that jumping and dazzling footwork—Skinny Minnie Fishtail movement for sure. I enrolled.

Somatically viewed, beginning ballet as an adult was not the best idea. Because I started twenty years later than most ballet students, I had to force muscles and tendons and joints into turned-out positions instead of having years to coax them there. There were times after class when walking was painful, but I loved ballet and soon was adding classes, continuing to dance after winter ended and after graduating from law school. It wasn't just the leaping or twirling or challenging gravity that got me to line up at the barre. Performing a movement over and over, sculpting it to its essence, then running the cloth of practice over it until it gleamed made my whole being hum.

I had seen Makarova dance. I watched in a trance, mesmerized by the poetry her arms and legs and torso created. I too wanted to write poetry with my body. "Ballet is a dance executed by the human soul," Alexander Pushkin said. When I danced, I felt that truth.

I started ballet with no idea how strenuous it was. Grace always looks effortless from an audience seat. Although my muscles stopped screaming after I went through enough barre exercises to convince them it was adapt or die, I panted during jump sequences. One day, I noticed a woman in class breathing normally after *grand jetés*. Her secret, I found out, was running.

"I do a mile every day," she told me. "It really helps with my wind."

I restarted and then increased my sidewalk loops. Before long, I was gobbling miles and shaving minutes from a newly acquired mile time. I entered races, 10k became my favorite distance. Eventually, to no one's surprise but mine, muscles shortened and tightened by running refused to lengthen for ballet without pain that lasted well beyond class.

When I found myself negotiating for more cortisone than my doctor thought I should have after yet another dance injury, I realized I would have to leave ballet. Although my mind, heart, and soul were ballet-compatible, my body wasn't. Despite wrapping before class and icing afterward, I couldn't prevent the myriad *itises* and *isms* resulting from my lack of symmetry and tight muscles. After I stopped dancing, I began having a recurring nightmare in which I was auditioning for Sugar Plum while George Balanchine watched me dance. I danced so far above myself, so flawlessly and passionately, that I was sure the role was mine. When the music stopped, Balanchine said, "My dear, you should be a lawyer." He was right, but in my heart of hearts, I wanted to be Sugar Plum taking the stage to magical celesta music.

I missed dancing in a mirrored studio, stretching with other dancers on a wooden floor, all of us awaiting the two hand claps that signaled the beginning of class. I missed exercises at the barre and hearing the beautiful French terms for them: *plié, ronde de jambe, arabesque.* I missed trying to perfect each small movement and watching the growing triangle of perspiration that appeared on my leotard below my shoulder blades as I did—confirmation of effort. I missed the moment when, tottering on one leg, the other stretched out behind me, my struggling muscles found center and internal balance. I missed the all-out physicality of the jump sequences. I missed the purposed practice of grace. But, mostly, I missed a way to let my soul shine through my shell of a body.

5

Boat Ballet

I am a failed road mystic. My mind chatters when I run. I think about how my body feels: tight, light, heavy, tired. What I have to do, what I've done, the morality of getting out of what I don't want to do. Why I didn't wear a jacket, why I did. Emmy Award-winning responses to things people have said to me days before. What I am going to eat next. That might explain why runner's high eludes me. But even if running hadn't put me on a path to enlightenment, it had gotten me moving again, a better place than where I had been. I kept running.

Then one day, as I hurried through a department store on my way to somewhere else, I glanced at a wall of televisions all tuned to the same channel. Muscular women in long boats sat one behind the other, each woman holding a long oar with both hands. I walked to within inches of the television screens as if I had been summoned. I heard a question asked in French: "*Etes-vous pret?*" It was as though the question, "Are you ready?" had been asked of me. I think I answered, *I am*. For what, I had no idea, but my answer was given with life-changing conviction.

Then I heard "*Partez*," a starter's gun fired, and the women exploded into rhythmic movement. There were sound effects as well—*kachunk* as the oars moved, and grunting as the women moved backward and forward in the boat. Each boat's ensemble executed its choreography with strength and perfect timing. It seemed like ballet in its grace, fluidity, and harmony of movement, but there was intensity and repetition, almost body as percussion, not present in ballet, yet somewhere in memory.

I had to row. It was as clear as my late-night direction: *Run.* There were no physical similarities between me and the women in that boat, yet I sensed an identity of spirit. I belonged in a rowing shell—my life's purpose revealed to me on a television screen in a discount department store.

What had not been revealed was how to find a way to row. Although I lived in a city built parallel to a river, the two had been estranged for years by a lattice of highways. It was difficult to even get to the river, and I had never seen anyone rowing on it. But a woman I ran with told me about seeing a flyer at her gym looking for adults interested in crew. I showed up at the boathouse one blustery Saturday morning in March in response to the notice. That there was no ice on the river was probably due to the cutting effect of whitecaps.

There are moments that make me believe love is simply a piercing of the heart with no will involved. Seeing a rowing shell up close for the first time was one of those moments for me. A white whale of a boat, about sixty feet long, it rested on carpet-covered metal arms protruding from the wall of the boathouse. The coach started our orientation by naming the parts of the boat and showing us where the oars were kept. The oars, each about twelve feet long, reminded me of a stand of Sequoias. Surrounded by equipment that looked like it was meant for giants, I should have felt small, reduced. Instead, I had a sense of being sheltered.

On the river, in an open boat, on that cold, windy, March day, I shivered the entire time despite the multiple layers of clothing I wore. To manipulate the oar handle, I had to remove my mittens. Within minutes, my fingers were numb and stayed that way the entire time we were out on the water.

We didn't go far. The coxswain, a jockey-sized man who had rowed years before in college, called for the *stern four* to row. Oars clashed as everybody rowed. The coxswain then called for *bow four* to row. Oars clashed again, no one understanding yet that in a boat you are a number associated with bow or stern, and if your number isn't called on to row, you sit at attention, helping to balance the boat. Voice now shrill, the coxswain yelled for us to *weigh enough*. We kept rowing, oars clashing. Not until the coxswain yelled *stop* did we cease rowing. I sat at my station, moved forward when the person in front of me did, struggled to extract my oar from water that sucked it down, and wondered if the rapture I felt was a natural talent for rowing.

Not often, and seemingly at random, all eight oars dipped into the river at the same time and moved together. When they did, I felt power and rhythm and the sweet glide that followed. There was a rightness to this movement. Something familiar but distant had been recalled.

6

Initiation

After we carried the boat back into the boathouse and placed it carefully on its rack, I ran to my car, started the engine, and moved the temperature dial to maximum heat. Even with hot air blasting from all the vents, I couldn't stop shivering. Feeling in my fingers wasn't restored until I dunked two digits at a time into a cup of coffee instead of drinking it. Not returning to row never occurred to me.

I had an open invitation to go back. As the coach locked the boathouse door, he said, "If you want to row, be here Monday morning at 5:30." I was ecstatic. I was going to get a chance to go out in the boat again. All I had to do was show up before dawn.

I am not a morning person, a fact that had gotten trampled in my excitement. Getting up at 7:30 a.m. on a workday was a hardship for me. On weekends, with no alarm claxoning me to consciousness, I might sleep until noon. Sleep had become the line I drew against the world. I loved going there, hated leaving.

But I was determined. Sunday night, I set my alarm for 5:15 a.m., estimating I could make the drive in ten minutes. Throwing on sweats would only take a minute or two, another thirty seconds for brushing my teeth, a minute for inserting contact lenses, and I'd have an extra minute and thirty seconds to spare before starting the car.

Donning sweats softened by wear and washing, dressing for warmth and mobility rather than the right mix of professional, yet feminine and fashionable, and dispensing with makeup made me feel I was starting a new life as a different person. I was the only driver on roads that I knew would be in gridlock in two hours. I sang "On the Road Again" during the drive. It felt like I was lighting out for the territory.

Out on the river, the coxswain kept us fully informed of our technique faults. Addressed by number only, I was cloaked in anonymity, which I learned could be forfeited by repeat rowing transgressions. "Who's three?" the coxswain would ask after a series of technique errors on my part. Someone in the boat always volunteered my name. I worked hard to achieve an error-free stroke and regain anonymity, but there was no formal instruction, no correction offered for errors that had been pointed out. I felt like a puppy trying to figure out what would get me a biscuit instead of a jerk on the leash.

My experience with boats before I began rowing had been a beamy eighteen-foot sailboat and a solo canoe about bathtub width. To me, the two-foot-wide eight-person shell felt narrow and tippy. Although an eight is the Queen Mary of shells in terms of stability, I didn't know that then. Whenever the eight rolled a little to one side or the other, I thought I was going over. Flipping an eight is such an unusual occurrence that news of the event is met with incredulity, followed by "How?" It can be done, but you have to try hard. Before I knew that, I felt so precarious in the eight that every time it dipped slightly, I gripped my oar as though it were a roller-coaster bar.

The coxswain called this rolling "down," followed by location: starboard or port. I inferred that "down" was not a good thing, and that we were supposed to do something about it. I had no idea what that might be, though. Later, I learned that rowers are supposed to keep the boat on an even keel by synchronizing body and hand movements. It takes an experienced crew to keep oar handle and body tracing and retracing the kinesthetic path where the boat is balanced. We were not an experienced crew. I had never rowed before, and neither had most of the people in the eight. It was everything I could do to extract my oar from the water at the finish and lower the blade into the water at the catch at the same time everybody else did. Meanwhile, the boat rocked like a cradle in a tree bough. Eventually, I learned that down on starboard or port was a call to raise or lower hands, not a signal to pass the life jackets.

Over the next few weeks, most of the initial crew drifted away. It wasn't difficult to understand why. My hands blistered, I got drenched with icy water from motorboat wakes, sliced a finger on the seam of the boat and bled the whole time I was rowing. I shrugged all this off because Canon 1 of the Rowers' Code is *Rowers are inured to physical discomfort.* Plus, I liked the honesty. In ballet, I had learned to hide the cost of effort, smile through pain. In the boat, effort and pain were undisguised, expected, part of rowing. Grunt, and the whole boat grunted with you. I was proud that my blisters were in the right places, on my fingers and the upper ridges of my palms, evidence that I was holding my oar handle correctly.

I was obliviously in love. I wakened at 5:15 every morning so I could be out on the water in the boat, concentrating on fast hands away, slow slide, squaring up early, synchronizing my stroke with everyone else's. Rowing was ensemble dance to me, the whole greater than the parts, self-subsumed in purpose. I was one of eight blades emerging from the water, part of the moving thread of shoulders. The coach said we were expected to die at our oar if it came to that. It was supposed to be a joke. But I was ready. Nothing would have made me happier than rowing martyrdom. A part of me knew this was crazy. I didn't care. I wanted to be nowhere but on the water, doing nothing but plying my oar, getting good, getting strong, dancing full out.

I progressed from "catching crabs," getting my blade stuck in the water, to a relatively clean stroke. I thought my technique had improved when the coxswain singled out my number for correction no more than any other number. I was never singled out for praise, but nobody was. Rowing appeared to be a positive-feedback-free activity. I assumed I was doing everything right unless the coxswain told me otherwise.

I had a mission: row perfectly, row hard, move the boat. I noticed that the boat moved better at higher cadences and full power. After rowing, I'd come off the water exhausted but enervated. I mainlined rowing.

7

Paradise Lost

By late April, we were rowing far upriver at high cadences. I put everything I had into those practices, determined to hold nothing back. I was usually seated in the back of the boat toward the bow, a scenic overlook. Seeing those blades emerging from the water together, moving in unison at the same height above the water, dipping and pulling at the same time, acted on me like a battle drum calling my heart to respond.

I started hearing about the June regatta. The boathouse and rowing club were part of the city's plan to promote interest in the riverfront—interest meaning development: condominiums, restaurants, marinas. Not content to seed interest and wait for an economic cloudburst, the city decided to jumpstart the anticipated riverfront resurrection by sponsoring a major regatta.

The usual gestation period for forming a club, acquiring boats, and building a boathouse is elephantine. Typically, when some critical membership level is reached, a used rowing shell is purchased—nothing as pricey as almost new, but usually second- or third-owner used. Years down the road, a boathouse may be financed and built.

But the city didn't want to wait for that process to take place. Its rowing club was like a builder's lawn. To get developers interested in the riverfront, the rowing grass had to be lush in days: club as chia plant. That's where the crew I was part of came in. Our boat was not only expected to compete with the best rowers the Northeast had to offer at the June regatta, but win.

In May, as the regatta loomed, young men who weren't part of our crew started showing up at the boathouse in the mornings. Each new guy, they showed up one at a time, would stand aloof. When the coach arrived, he would ask the new guy if he was so-and-so, shake his hand, and start the head count. The new guy was always included in the lineup for that morning.

The trickle of new guys was steady. They were all experienced rowers, and the coach deferred to their programs ("Is this the way you did it at your college?" "What do you think we should do this morning?"). It wasn't just the coach; we all deferred to the new guys. They were race-hardened, they had technique, and having them in the boat would make us betters rowers and help us win the regatta.

Boat arithmetic changed. Every morning, at least twelve people showed up. After asking for volunteers willing to be bumped from the boat, the coach would look over the group that remained, point to someone, and assign a seat number. If you got a number, you were in the boat that morning. If not, you were in your car on the way home.

At first it seemed that, except for the *nouveau*-shows, an effort was made to balance rejection: if you got a number on Monday, you wouldn't get one on Wednesday. Because rain was a surefire means of reducing attendance at practice, I started to relish bad weather. I hated arriving at 5:30 a.m. only to be headed for home at 5:45 a.m. I had to constantly remind myself that having experienced rowers in the boat was a learning opportunity.

After a few weeks of point-and-number selection, I noticed that the new guys were given seats first, followed by men from the club, with women chosen last to fill any seats left. I observed this pattern a few more times before checking with one of the other women regulars to make sure I wasn't imagining sidelining based on gender.

The discrimination, it turned out, was deliberate. There was an inside source: my rowing colleague's boyfriend was a confidant of the coach. He told her that the city wanted to make a good showing in the regatta, which was why the boat was going out with a mostly male crew and why the new guys had been recruited for the boat. Things would be different after the regatta, he promised.

My rowing friend and I talked. We had a lot of time to do that because we weren't rowing and didn't have to be at work for hours. The regatta was only a few weeks away. We wanted the club to be successful. We believed that after the regatta, everything would go back to the way it had been.

The day after the regatta, I showed up for practice looking forward to rowing after a weeks-long hiatus. Men were chosen for seats first; women were still fill-ins for any seats left. Nothing had changed, which led to more conversations with my rowing friend about what to say and how to say it. We didn't want to be confrontational. We were all part of the same club and felt sure that the promised post-regatta reset just needed a nudge.

We finally asked the coach, "Do women have any chance to be regulars in the boat?" He shrugged and splayed his hands in the universal gesture of helplessness.

I found myself losing the daily seat lottery more and more. Women started dropping out of the boat. Getting a seat in the boat if you were female had become a random event. But all those traits I learned in Catholic school—perseverance in the face of adversity, maintaining hope in times of despair, believing as a matter of faith: traits useful during martyrdom and pretty much nothing else—kicked in. Maybe some stubbornness too. And not wanting to go cold turkey.

I had lost ballet, found rowing by chance, and was not about to have the feeling I got being out on the water taken from me by a little garden-variety sex discrimination. My friend and I talked to the coach again. More shrugs. It was reported back to her by her boyfriend, who had become part of the permanent crew, that we were considered troublemakers.

One morning, while waiting to learn if I would get a seat assignment, I rehearsed my argument on the injustice of it all to a nonexistent tribunal with jurisdiction to right life's wrongs and watched the scullers arrive. Unlike the rowers, scullers did not stand around waiting for a coach to appear, waiting for a coxswain, waiting to find out who would be chosen for a seat in the boat. Like barn cats, tolerated but not fed, their comings and goings not noticed, they simply walked past the knot of waiting rowers, entered the boathouse, and came out headtopping their sculls. Within minutes, each sculler had launched from the dock.

I'd look at the river as I drove home, unboated, and see the scullers out on the water, solitary and small, a needle flotilla moving upriver. I still thought of scullers as odd people pursuing an odd activity, not one holding any inherent fascination for me. I was a rower. But as I got fewer and fewer opportunities to go out in the boat, "rower" was becoming an honorific.

I cannot properly account for my decision to bypass the rigged seat lottery by taking up sculling. It was not a rational decision. I did not take my observation of the scullers getting out on the water while I wanted to and couldn't and conclude that they had a more efficient means of achieving my goal. I did not gather information upon which to base a decision. I did not compare the costs and benefits of sculling versus rowing. I couldn't have; I didn't know what they were. I had never sat in a scull, didn't know the technique, and had no idea how I would get access to a scull. I could say it was intuitive logic, but I don't remember anything even remotely logical or intuitive going on. What I do remember was a mind flash, a *before*, heavy with uncertainty and helplessness, and an *after* of clarity. My Eureka moment was probably created by neurotransmitters blowing up in my brain, strained beyond limit by my determination to hold on to the feeling I got when out on the water. Thought plus will equals mystical experience.

My family would have characterized my decision as "dishing out your own Jell-O." Canned fruit cocktail suspended in red Jell-O was frequently dessert when I was growing up. Sometimes my mother sneaked bananas into green Jell-O or put pineapple in orange Jell-O, but that fruit was never as coveted as the sugar-hardened pear, peach, and grapes in red Jell-O. Distribution of that fruit was not uniform, however. I was old enough to serve myself from the green bowl we knew as the Jell-O bowl and I always spooned from the fruit-laden veins. My sister, younger by two and a half years, had her portion doled. One night, she clamored for the right to serve herself, shouting down adult misgivings regarding her ability to spoon from one bowl and transport to another. We watched her scoop into the green bowl, bring up a quivering red mound, and plop the Jell-O on to the floor before it reached her dish. "Dishing out your own Jell-O" became family shorthand for insisting you can do something when you have no idea whether you can or not.

Just as my sister knew that if she wanted a shot at the fruit cocktail, she had to take control of the serving spoon, I knew that if I wanted to guarantee I'd get out on the water in a boat, I'd have to take up sculling. I thought sculling would be like rowing but with seven fewer people. There was an ad for a sculling school in the rowing magazine I subscribed to. I would go and learn to scull. Problem solved. Jell-O dished.

8

Floating

I researched the skills needed for sculling and learned they were: balance, coordination, aerobic capacity, and ability to swim. Busy putting mental markers on my sculling card, excited that I had every number called out, I didn't wonder why knowing how to swim was important. A few books mentioned swimming in water safety chapters, which I skimmed, thinking it had nothing to do with mastery of sculling technique and so wouldn't be on the final. Besides, I could swim; my college transcript said so.

My churning style, reminiscent of a tightly twisted rubber band sputtering loose, was good enough to pass the college freshman swim test—one lap, any combination of strokes— exempting me from a semester of icicled hair in a Northeast winter. I could swim as far as a held breath would take me, which wasn't far. Then I had to stand up and gulp air. If I couldn't stand because the water was deeper than five feet, I needed to grab hold of something so I could float until I caught my breath. I tried to master breathing while swimming, but no matter what I did, I ended up swallowing water. Swallowing water might have been considered an inevitable part of correct breathing technique, but it felt too much like drowning to me.

I had come to my sputtering, churning style after failing beginner swimming lessons when I was nine years old. The Red Cross offered those lessons as part of its water safety program and used a pool with water that was so cold it felt like it had come from a glacier. In addition, the pool was deeply shaded during the hour-long session. Beginners like me who could not swim gathered in the shallow end of the pool, where the water was three feet deep before it dropped off, without warning, to four feet and then five feet and deeper. When I stood in the three-foot area, the combination of cold water and shade chilled my upper body. If I submerged my body, I'd drift too close to the four-foot drop-off and have to splash and sputter my way back to safety. I remained in a state of frozen tension for the duration of the session. Between the Scylla and Charybdis of freeze or drown, I never relaxed.

Floating, deemed the foundation for swimming at the time because it was seen as so easy and natural that anyone could do it, was the first lesson. Once you could float, it was a simple matter to add arm and leg movement. Or so the theory went.

The instructor placed her hands under my torso and then removed them, expecting that I'd stay on top of the water, but I sank. She tried repositioning me and letting go several times with the same result—I sank. I didn't understand why I couldn't float when the other children in my class not only could but had progressed to swimming. I knew only that I had failed at something easy, natural—something that it seemed everybody, except me, could do.

Eventually, I learned to swim on my own. Extending my doggie paddle from a few seconds of thrashing in place to traveling a short distance convinced me that the water would hold me up, to some extent. But I kept my head lifted like a retriever and couldn't make much headway.

Although I tried floating on my back, it was mostly an exercise in fighting off panic. As soon as I retracted my legs, my body started to sink. When I felt water lapping my forehead, I had to override my panicked impulse to stand up and instead make minute adjustments: tilt my head back, thrust chin and neck skyward, tighten my buttocks, and raise my pelvis. As my head sank lower, I had to fight off panic and readjust my head and pelvis again. For me, floating was all about tension, not energy-conserving relaxation required for a sustainable survival technique.

But once in a while, after I tilted my head back, I'd feel the sun on my face and shoulders and wonder if it was sending warmth to me because it knew I was cold and scared. Then, wanting nothing but feeling that heat working its way inward to bone, I'd relax and let the water cradle and rock me gently. I'd lose track of time and boundaries. It seemed I was in the sky with the clouds I was watching. I tried to re-create the feeling of being supported, carried papoose-style on the back of the water, secure in its strength to hold me up, comfortable in the softness that washed over me, but I couldn't summon it. Only when I lost awareness of everything but warmth and rocking would it come.

Instead of gutter-grabbing, a tired swimmer is supposed to tread water, which, like floating, is presented as an easy, relaxing way to stay above the surface. I'd jump into the deep end of a pool, panic at total immersion, flail until I broke through the surface, and then have to move my legs at spinning cadence to keep my head above water. It seemed I lacked buoyancy.

Eventually, I learned how to breaststroke and sidestroke with my head above water and that was how I passed the one lap college swimming test. Floating was sustained tension, and treading water was like pedaling a unicycle as fast as I could. I couldn't swim far, tread water for long, or count on being able to float. I ventured into deep water only when there was something in proximity that I could grab hold of.

It wasn't until I was out on the water in a scull that I was able to decode the information I had been given about swimming as being essential for that activity. Knowing how to swim was not just about survival, it was more about an easy, comfortable relationship with water, a nonchalance as to whether you were in the boat or the water. One reason children learn to scull so easily is that whether they are in the boat or in the water makes no difference: it's all play to them. Not to me. When I decided to begin sculling, my relationship with deep water was frissoned with fear.

9
Sculling School

My trip to sculling school was over two-lane roads with maddeningly slow speed limits. Stuck behind obedient drivers who did not pass in no-passing zones or exceed the speed limit, I had time to look at the green fields on either side of roads that went on forever—mountains behind them, cows in the foreground—and disparage the pastoral beauty for its lack of four-lane highways. I wanted to get where I was going as fast as I could. As far as I was concerned at that point in my life, journey meant nothing more than the fastest route to a destination.

Directions sent from the school mentioned a final turn on to a dirt road. I had never driven on a dirt road. "Dirt" did not equal "road" to me. I expected an unpaved spur of short duration, about driveway length, the school visible within a few seconds after turning. I turned off the paved road and drove in a cloud of brown dust trying to avoid rocks along the path. It was mid-June but unexpectedly hot. Sealed in a car without air conditioning, it felt even hotter.

There were houses along the road, and every time I saw one, sure that it must be part of the school, I'd turn into the driveway and look for a signboard with the school's name. But it was always someone's home. I kept going, convinced that I was on the wrong road, lost, would never find the school but would eventually come to a gingerbread house with a resident witch. Panic rose with the dust. Miles after my turn, the school came into view.

The school was a motley cluster of three buildings: two three-story dormitories and a one-story dining hall. The buildings were cinder block; the design functional. When I later learned that the school's architectural history had been juvenile reform camp, I wasn't surprised.

My accommodation for the week was a musty room that I shared with another woman, bathroom and showers down the hall. I checked in and gathered on the dock with the twenty other people in the class, most of whom had never sculled before.

Our first lesson was capsizing and boat re-entry. The premise was that if you knew how to get back into the boat, you wouldn't worry about falling out of it, freeing you to focus on learning to scull. It was a great foundational idea and reminded me of my college ice-skating instruction that built confidence by teaching how to recover from inevitable falls. I, for whom floating was an act of will, daughter of a mother who could not float, descendant of people for whom immersion in water was an untoward and to-be-avoided-at-all-costs event, walked out on that dock as though I had no disqualifying piscine past, ready to acquire confidence.

One of the coaches sculled a couple of strokes from the dock, raised one oar higher than the other, and capsized. That was how easy it was to leave the boat. He then demonstrated how to get back into the boat. The formula was hold both oar handles together in one hand, push up from the deck with your free hand, and then swing your body into the boat. It looked so easy. I mentally rehearsed the steps while watching each of my classmates fall into the water and pop back into the boat.

I was last. I pushed away from the dock and raised one oar but the boat didn't go over. A good omen, I thought. Coached from the dock to take both hands off the oars, I lifted my hands and capsized.

The water was icy. I wanted to get out of it immediately. I wasn't worried—three easy steps, and I'd be on my way back to the dock. Step one was not as depicted in the demo, however. One oar had gone under the boat when it rolled me out. I dived under the boat to free it and, when I did, the other oar nose-dived into the water. "Hold on to them" came the too-late instruction from the dock. I finally managed to place both oars in the outrigger position and hold on to them with my left hand.

Ready for step two: the one-handed push-up. I pushed against the deck of the boat with my right hand. My shoulders came out of the water but not the rest of me. I pushed again. Same result. I felt colder.

"Kick hard at the same time you push," the coach urged. I did, but while the effort brought my shoulders a little higher, it wasn't enough to twist and flop me into the boat. I started to tire. I had been in cold water for what felt to me like a long time, all the while expending energy. My breath started to come quicker. More instructions shouted from the dock: "Push yourself over. Push harder. Try again," and, finally, "Just swim the boat to the dock."

Instead of acquiring confidence so I'd relax and wouldn't worry about falling out of the boat, I learned that capsizing was easy, re-entry impossible. Because I couldn't get back into the boat, I concluded that I should do nothing to jeopardize staying in it, that my every movement, every breath, should have one purpose: keeping me in the boat. My backup plan was to stay close to land so I could swim the boat to shore with a few strokes and have a platform for re-entry in case I failed to stay in the boat.

As I was to learn later, in sculling there is the plan and what actually happens, almost always two wildly different events. My plan to get back into a capsized boat by standing in shallow water for re-entry depended on proximity to shoreline, not easy to come by on the lake. Most of the shore was privately owned, off limits to scullers. In addition, the lake was deep—sixty feet in some places. There was no place where I wouldn't be in over my head if the boat deposited me in the water. Not that I already wasn't in over my head, metaphorically speaking.

10

Slip Slidin'

Technically, a scull is any boat propelled by one rower using two oars, but the term commonly refers to a long, narrow boat about twenty-six-feet long and ten to twelve inches wide. Single and scull are often used interchangeably.

The school had a boathouse full of singles and a complement of recreational shells: shorter, wider, boats. I was assigned one of those learn-to-row recreational singles at the beginning of my week at sculling school. Stable and sensible, it was a veritable Dr. Scholl's of boats. I could have stayed with that boat for the entire week—or my life, for that matter. I was the one who asked to transfer to a racing scull.

I had gone to sculling school so I could get back out on the water; I assumed the kind of boat I used didn't matter. A scull is a scull; wool is as warm as cashmere. That's what I believed until I took one of the school's single sculls out for a spin.

Instruction was dockside: one coach presented theory, while another, in a single on the water, demonstrated. Watching the coaches execute a perfect catch or seemingly effortless release was like seeing ballet dancers perform with elegance and grace.

As I watched these dockside demonstrations, I sensed that I was seeing the subtle intricacies that make up the art of sculling.

After the lesson, students trooped up a hill to the boathouse, carried assigned boats down to the dock, and launched to designated water classrooms on the lake. The departing singles, piloted by experienced scullers, looked like a squadron of fighter planes as they headed to the end of the lake. They were longer than my assigned craft and sleek, not stubby.

At the end of the morning session on the second day, as the singles returned, I asked a coach if I could sit in one and paddle around the dock. My request was a whim, a fantasy that, somehow, by sitting in a single, some of its quicksilver beauty would rub off on me.

"Sure," he said. If I had been a mind reader, I might also have heard *Knock yourself out, kid.*

I didn't expect how light the single would feel compared to my heavy boat or how silky smooth it would feel as it slipped through the water or how long the glide between strokes would be. I did not expect to get hooked on the lure of glide based on a few minutes of sitting in a single, but my crazy, wild heart chose that moment to make a break for it.

There was no glide in my stable boat. I pulled on the oars, traveled a short distance, pulled again. Plunk, move, remove. Up the lake, down the lake. Nothing but effort, a metaphor for my life—Thursday's Child working hard. No glide, no grace.

Maybe that was why, as I moved my oars gently, tentatively through water and felt that glide, I asked if I could switch from my assigned boat to a single. Glide seemed a blessing from the universe, respite from perpetually rolling a heavy rock up a mountain.

When the coach asked me why I wanted to switch, I said, "The boat I'm in is clunky. There's no glide. I want glide." I might have told him, had I known at the time, that I wanted to feel an expression of the universe's love—grace bestowed *just because*. A spiritual hug. No merit required. I believed it could happen, but it hadn't happened to me. It seemed I was on a merit system in which working hard might get me what I needed but never what I wanted. I thought that feeling glide between strokes was as close to grace as I'd ever get.

"Are you sure? Singles have glide, but they aren't as stable as the boat you are in now."

His admonition about a scull not being "as stable" as the wide, heavy boat I had been using caused me no consternation. Relief from unrelenting effort as manifested by glide was what I wanted. Trading a smidgen of stability for that seemed like a good exchange. I didn't know that another way to interpret "as stable" was through the prism of propensity: sculls are tippy and inclined to overturn; recreational singles are not.

Something about an upside-down scull connotes a return to a natural configuration. You can almost hear a contented "ahh" when it flips over. Unoccupied, a scull's semicircular hull needs girdling—structure for sustained upright posture. Occupied, a sculler's higher center of gravity affects the boat's balance and requires holding on to outrigger-like nine-foot oars on each side of the boat to stay upright. *Never let go of the oar handles* is a prime directive in sculling. It's simply good physics.

I looked at the scull alongside the dock, a craft that my brain hadn't categorized as a boat just a few months before, and then at my assigned boat. The scull, sleek and streamlined, was designed for speed; the recreational single, broad and stubby, was meant for safety, predictability. Although the scull was a descendant of beamy rowboats known as wherries, that kinship was unrecognizable to me as I compared the two boats.

The scull's evolution was rooted in commerce, competition, and cash. When London had few bridges spanning the Thames, wherries were used as water taxis to transport people and cargo across the river. Wagering by passengers as to which boats were fastest led to informal races and, eventually, sponsored ones. In 1715, the first Doggett's Coat and Badge Race was held. The official prize, a splendid red coat and silver arm badge, was coveted, but it was the substantial gambling winnings that motivated innovation to increase boat speed. Attaching an outrigger allowed for a narrower hull and longer oars, making the boats faster. The invention of the sliding seat followed, and the scull was born.

I had been assigned my stable boat based on the conventional wisdom that learning to scull in a wide, stubby boat would allow acquisition of technique without terror. Uninterrupted progress is assumed upon transfer to a narrower, less stable boat. Many who have followed that method will attest that it works. But there are others who claim that the benign experience of sculling in a stable boat gives a false sense of security and only defers a reckoning with balance. I knew nothing of this teaching methodology debate; all I knew was that I wanted glide, something that only a scull is capable of bestowing.

Going back to my Barcalounger of a boat was the sensible, rational decision, I knew that. But I had been making sensible, rational choices my whole life and not one had conferred the brief moments of joy that feeling glide between strokes had.

A scull is not user-friendly, but I was willing to go out in one if it meant a chance to experience lightness, glide, the blessings of a benevolent universe. It never occurred to me to ask what questers in search of the grail of glide needed to pack for the journey.

11

Sculling

During the dockside lessons held twice a day, the coaches simplified sculling as three components: catch, drive, release. Plunking both oars in the water is the catch. Moving them through the water is the drive. Taking them out is the release. Plunk, move, remove—as easy as amplifying the sound of one hand clapping.

One oar is held in the fingers of each hand, thumb pressing against the end of the handle. Fingers exert holding pressure; thumbs provide horizontal pressure. Ideal pressure is the force necessary to hold a robin's egg without breaking the shell.

For the catch, arms move first, toward the stern, one hand slightly ahead of the other. As arms move, the pelvis tilts forward. Knees begin to bend as the oar handles pass over flattened legs. Body starts to slide forward, and fingers rotate oar handles in the oarlocks from parallel to perpendicular. Torso meets legs, hands lift, blades meet water.

For the drive, body-as-spring uncoils: legs first, then the back. Straight arms bend as they are drawn toward the torso, elbows wing out. A slight downward motion of the wrist releases blades from the water. As oars move bow-ward for another catch, blades ride inches above the water. Movement is continuous but at different speeds: hands move fast, body moves no faster than the boat.

Technique is following that formula, but beyond technique, behind the metaphysical veil, when body and boat move as one, when everything is light, when it feels like you are floating through time, there is, as George Pocock—who crafted some of the fastest, most beautiful crew shells ever built—observed, a "touching [of] the divine ... which is your soul." Coaches can teach you hand position, arm movement, leg drive, but no one can teach you how to catch that curl of time and ride.

"Relax," the coaches would say when they spotted my hands squeezing the oar handles. After they had moved on to the next sculler, I resumed my death grip. I couldn't relax. As soon as I moved my oars, I was at the top of a Ferris wheel, rocking. I was always conscious that I was precariously balanced, that I had no safety net. Over deep, shoreless water, my heart beat at hummingbird rhythm as I pincered my oar handles. Instead of learning to scull, which is about flow and blurring boundaries between boat and water, I was teaching myself how to stay in the boat.

"Your hands are the boat. Whatever your hands are doing, the boat is doing," a coach told us. Oar handles overlap as you draw them toward you and push them away. To deal with the overlap, one rigger is set higher than the other, and you are taught to send one hand slightly ahead of the other. The convention in the United States is left hand precedes the right hand. Unschooled and impatient, both of my hands wanted to lead. They'd collide with an impact that would have sent the oars flying out of my hands and me into the water if I hadn't been holding on to them like a raptor with prey.

To avoid the crossover hand jam, I'd raise one hand. When I did this, the boat dipped to one side, making me fear it was prelude to a capsize. To correct this dive, I'd raise my other hand, initiating a dive to the other side. I recited the hand sequence: "left ahead of right," and when that didn't work, preferred raking skin off my knuckles to rocking and dipping.

The only thing that brought my hands in any proximity to each other was keeping my eyes on them at all times. But full-time supervision of my hands meant I couldn't turn and look toward my bow to see where I was going. So I devised my own method of navigating: looking down through the clear water to the bottom of the lake where I could see vegetation, rocks, tree limbs. Underwater plants signaled shallow water. When I could no longer see vegetation, I knew I was over deeper water. When I looked through the clear water to the lake bottom, it felt like I was high in the sky flying above a miniaturized world below. While the thought of falling out of the boat terrified me, falling out of the sky did not. One of the few times I relaxed in the boat that week was when I was so focused on the water world under me that I forgot I was in a tippy, capricious craft.

Every morning, after our dockside instruction, the scullers, who ranged in experience from people like me who had never been in a scull to competitive scullers who were there for a little fine-tuning before racing season, were divided into three groups for on-water instruction: end of lake, middle of lake, dock. No explanation was given for what made you an end-of-lake sculler or dock sculler, but having been in a secretly ranked group before that, I thought I knew the basis.

In my first-grade class, there were three reading groups: Blessed Mother, Saint Joseph, and Infant Jesus. The group names were not supposed to reveal who could read and who couldn't, but we all knew. We knew because when called on to read aloud, Infant Jesus readers sounded out S-p-o-t over and over without being able to recognize the word. The Blessed Mother readers, on the other hand, usually had to be told to take their seats before they whizzed through the entire reader.

It was just as easy to decode lake location nomenclature. Good scullers convened at the end of the lake because they could get there fast. Middle-of-the-lake scullers were steady but not as fast. Dock scullers were slow, unstable, and unpredictably inept. I had been a Blessed Mother reader, impatient at the time with those learning to read at a slower pace. As a low-status dock sculler, I was beginning to understand what it was like to climb up the sheer face of a learning curve.

Like my fellow dock scullers, I serpentined as I sculled, my signature wake a half-helix. Because our circles and tacks from shore to shore, although interesting, presented a navigation hazard, the coaches added instruction in piloting and collision prevention to our curriculum.

I understood piloting to be like land surveying: line up the boat's bow with a destination point and sight from there to a sternward point of reference. Sighting from bow to stern would get you from A to B in a straight line, but what it wouldn't do was keep you from crashing into a rock or another boat in your path. That involved collision prevention, another skill to master.

Collision prevention required turning your head to look behind you because in a scull you face what you are leaving, like riding backward on a train. But turning your heavy head, whose estimated weight is ten to eleven pounds, is enough to throw the boat off balance—minutely, if you are experienced and skilled. But if, like me, shoulders follow that head, and skill is nothing but a pipe dream, then turning-and-looking is one complex task too many.

I felt like someone had set batons I was just learning to twirl on fire. When I twisted around in the boat, my unsupervised hands moved, the boat lurched, and I momentarily stopped breathing. I vowed that if I didn't capsize, I would be good, which, freely translated, meant I would do something I didn't want to do, something that made me miserable. Years of deal-making with God had prepared me for ongoing negotiations with divinities—a skill, it turned out, as essential to sculling as feathering oars.

A head race, a point-to-point competition against the clock, was held on the last day of sculling school. My goal during the race, as it had been all week, was to stay in the boat. I succeeded.

12

Opacity

Before going to sculling school, I had joined a rowing club on a different river that was a half-hour drive from where I lived. I had misgivings about the commute, but it was the only alternative to my ex-club, from which I considered myself divorced. The new club had a boathouse, boats, access to a river—everything I thought I needed.

The morning after I returned from my week of sculling instruction, I drove there, ready to take out one of the sculls available to members. No one was there when I unlocked the barn-sized boathouse doors, slid them open, and entered. Sunlight filtered through one of the clear roof panels, creating a shaft of light from ceiling to gravel floor. It looked like the heavenly light in Renaissance paintings: pale but piercing. Wooden Kaschpers, Kings, and Pococks were suspended on slings high in the rafters above. Wood, oil, and resin, the smell of craft, devotion to equipment, and belief that chaos can be held in abeyance through proper maintenance and attention to detail permeated the boathouse. I felt like an intruder in a holy place.

While I was standing in the back of the boathouse studying a hand-drawn map of the river, a man and woman entered.

They each removed singles from racks and left without seeming to notice I was there.

I chose the same model single I had been using at school from the selection of club boats and headed down to the dock. Carrying the club single down to the dock was a struggle. At sculling school, there had always been someone willing to help with transport in return for like assistance. The boat was heavy, balance transitory. Bow and stern took turns diving toward the ground.

The man and woman I had seen in the boathouse were on the ping-pong-table-sized dock when I arrived. I managed to put my boat in the water but wasn't sure of the etiquette for launching interaction. Eyes straight ahead, speak, do not speak, discuss weather-related topics only? Given my low tolerance for socially awkward situations, I introduced myself.

She told me her name; he never spoke. I asked if there was any part of the river I should avoid. She said something about abutments and then, pointing to my boat rocking gently at the dock, asked how many times I had been out in a single. I told her I had just come back from a week at sculling school. "Hmm," she said, without giving me an interpretive clue as to what she thought my chances of survival were with just a week of sculling instruction. She climbed into her boat, gave her male companion, already sitting in his, a signal to push off, and then, with a "Good luck" to me, left the dock. They quickly disappeared from sight. I was glad they were gone; I didn't want witnesses for my launch. I preferred that any capsize during launching remain a secret between me and the dock.

I surveyed the river from where I stood. A rocky barrier island separating the main part of the river from the opposite shoreline ran upriver as far as I could see. A yellow-hulled motorboat, anchored about thirty feet from the dock, prevented me from starting out along the dockside shoreline. Motorboats zoomed up and down the middle of the river. Except for coaching launches, there had been no motorboats on the sculling school lake, and now the noise, speed, and deeply troughed wakes frightened me into deciding to stay out of the channel. Hugging the dockside shoreline whenever I could get close enough, staying out of the channel, navigating by below-water signposts, and practicing abutment avoidance, whatever that was, seemed my only options.

As soon as I sat in the boat, something felt wrong. I checked for leaks and made sure my oarlocks were facing the right direction. I could see the bottom of the silty river through the shallow water around the dock. I pushed off, took a tentative stroke, and panicked. The river was opaque.

When I was eight, I took a half-hour piano lesson once a week after school in a convent parlor from which I could smell the nuns' dinner cooking. Playing the piano was easy. There were numbers under the notes that I matched to the keys. I settled into a routine of playing a piece, getting a gold star, and moving on to the next piece.

"Making amazing progress. She's well ahead of the other children," I heard the nun who taught beginner piano say to my mother one day after the lesson. My status as a musical prodigy came up in conversations my mother had with friends. Buying a piano was broached with my father.

And then I got a new piano book because I had zipped through all the pieces in my beginner book. Except this book did not have numbers written under the notes. I froze. Sister pointed at a note. I guessed discordantly wrong. After she asked me to name a few of the club-shaped sticks suspended in various locations throughout the lattice-like lines across the page, it became clear I was not a prodigy. "Cheating," Sister called it as she took away my new book and opened my old one to the beginning. "You'll never cheat like that again now, will you?"

But I had. I was now staring at the river as hard as I had stared at those indecipherable notes. I could not see past the brownish-green surface. My navigational adaptation, looking through clear water so I could stay in shallow areas, wouldn't work here. Without being able to see to the bottom, I had no way of telling how deep the water was. Without knowing that, I couldn't tell if it was all right to practice good technique because I could touch bottom if I capsized and have a platform to re-enter the boat or whether to risk nothing and abandon technique.

I had drifted too far from the dock to reach out and bring myself back to safety. I sensed that if I had been able to retreat, I would have never ventured out again. I lurched up the river, terrified every second. I didn't go far. When I got to a place where the river flared to bay dimensions, which I interpreted as meaning it also deepened to uncharted fathoms, I turned and headed back to the dock.

After I brought the boat alongside the dock, I clambered out, grateful to be someplace that didn't rock or shift. I sat on the dock for a while, afraid that my knees would buckle if I stood.

13

Spitfire Training

My father taught me when I was six that if your fighter plane is shot out from under you, you get back into another plane and fly into the wild blue yonder as soon as possible. He told me that was how the RAF trained pilots during World War II and was one of the reasons England won the Battle of Britain.

I understood that he was talking about me learning to ride a bike, not fly Spitfires. The training wheels had come off my two-wheeler that I had pedaled with fearlessness and now, without them, I couldn't balance, had fallen umpteen times, and wanted to give up. My father did not say, "Don't give up in frustration. Keep trying." He seldom used commands, prohibitions, or exhortations, figuring that his children would resist them, as did he. He believed that a gentle, reasonable approach was the path to behavioral change and that the right story was the most powerful way to communicate a lesson. The stories from which he drew lessons were of bravery, goodness, and eventual triumph. How could anyone not follow the Spitfire Way, especially a child who loved her father and did not want to disappoint him?

Just as I had gotten back on my bike when I was six. I went out again the following weekend in a club single—not because I was brave or optimistic; I wasn't either. My return was mostly because of that inculcation of RAF Spitfire pilot-training principles. Applied to my life, this meant that whenever something filled me with nameless dread and made me want to take to my bed and sleep for the duration of my life with the covers pulled over my head, I knew I had to get out there and face the terror instead. Sculling had begun to qualify as "nameless dread" for me.

The dock was pewter gray. I remember that and the rust-colored scabs where paint had worn away because I looked at them for such a long time while sitting in the boat. I checked and rechecked oarlocks, squirmed on the seat, not satisfied with my position, hoping I'd find something wrong that would prevent me from going out. Something attributable to equipment failure, not my lack of courage. In the end, I had to will myself to launch. I had learned to move at the end of an 8-count in ballet, exigencies of music and choreography trumping performance anxiety. *Five, six, seven.* I watched my left hand as though it might at the last moment betray my will and hold on to the dock. *Eight.* Push away. And if I had remembered to close the oarlock gates and had positioned the oarlock cylinders so they faced bow, I was still right-side up.

I used any excuse to not go out: too windy, too many motor boats, too tired, it might rain. I'd drive to the boathouse hoping that all the club singles were signed out. I could get my heart rate in my training zone, 170 to 180 beats per minute, just by thinking about going out in a scull.

When I did manage to slash through those dragons in my mind and get out on the river, I believed that my mental effort kept the boat afloat. I sat tense, determined, hands squeezing the oar handles. I recited the sequence of movement—*legs-backarms, armsbacklegs*—as I went up and down the slide, not trusting body memory. My sculling was jerky, uneven—nothing flowed. Coaching voices told me to *keep my head up, sit up straight, don't hesitate at the catch, don't rush the slide, loosen your death grip on the oar handles.* Besides being scared, I never felt I was doing anything right. I wondered if failure's tenses: I fail, I failed, I will fail—would be an inescapable loop.

I willed myself to continue going out. Nothing changed. There was lurching and fear and gratitude for landfall when my sojourn on the river had ended. I disciplined myself to go a little farther each time and eventually made it upriver to an island about a mile and a half from the dock.

I grew to love that island. It was a place to hide from the world, a place I felt safe. There was shoreline there, in case I needed it to get back into the boat, and tree branches overhanging the water for shade. I could count on calm water most of the time. The calm water and shoreline made this part of the river the place I risked practicing what I was afraid to try in the main channel. I felt when I set out from the dock that if I could get to my island refuge, I'd be okay.

Because I had made it there and back without capsizing, I became obsessed with retracing my exact passage. And the route wasn't all I obsessed about. I had to wear the same cap, the same sunglasses, bring the same water bottle. I believed ritual kept me afloat. I *knew* it couldn't be anything I did.

Other than when I was at the island, I never relaxed in the boat. The boat would tip to one side, my heart rate zoomed, and I'd bring the oars back to the safe outrigger position without having any idea what I had done to affect the boat's balance. I was scared all the time. The weight of unending effort wore on me.

The river was tricky. The cement buoys, rocks, logs, docks and other boats on it were all seemingly in a state of constant rearrangement. A log I had charted one day wouldn't be in the same place the next, and my anxiety about where it lay in wait to cripple my boat would start as soon as I approached the log-less spot. Sometimes I saw what I was about to hit just seconds beforehand. My mental state when on the water deteriorated to the point that I imagined the buoys had walkie-talkies, communicating my position to one another so they could call plays with different lineups. *Number 73, she's going to miss hitting you if you don't move to starboard ASAP.*

I was so occupied with looking behind me to avoid collisions that I hardly looked in front of me. Then one day, I happened to look at my stern and saw the "s" I had carved in the water with my wake and understood how I could look behind, see nothing in my path, and end up knocking at a channel marker's door. Until I saw my curving trail, I had no idea I was serpentining all over the river. To correct that, I began thinking of my boat as an arrow aimed at a target. I took deep pleasure in the straightness of that line I drew in the water with my boat and the knowledge that I was going where I intended. From then on, my wake guided me.

Watching the boat's brushstroke mesmerized me, making me forget that I couldn't see how deep the water below me was. My mind quieted. The thrumming *should* noises in my head were displaced by the plunk of blades locking into water, the click of oars turning, and the whirr of my seat moving up and down the metal track. I stopped watching my hands and listened to the boat moving through the water. The more I listened, the less I needed to see.

14

Inexorability

I bought a scull about a year after I returned from sculling school even though the club had boats for members' use: two singles known for their ability to survive crashes with logs, buoys, and docks, and an older wooden scull referred to as "Satan." Satan tossed its occupant as frequently as a bucking bronco.

At the club's annual dinner, I heard stories about Satan: "I was out one day, and the river was so calm you'd think you were rowing on a blanket. All of a sudden, a leaf fell in front of Satan's stern. Over I went."

"I never took a full breath while I was in Satan, just quick, quiet breaths through my nose. It seemed to work; I stayed in the boat. Then one day, a couple of feet from the dock, I forgot and breathed deeply. Probably in relief. Over I went."

Two reasons prompted me to buy my own single: I did not consider Satan an acceptable alternative if the other two boats were in use, and I had begun equating boat ownership with having your own running shoes.

I ordered the same model boat I used at the club. The biggest selling point for me was that I had so far managed to stay in it. What the boat lacked in initial stability, it more than made up for in secondary stability, offering a grace period of a second or so to restore equilibrium before the point of no return. When I checked the specifications before ordering, I saw that the single's width was twelve inches. Worried that my stern measured more than twelve inches and would hang over the sides of the boat, I sat on a ruler before placing my order to make sure I'd avoid at least that particular embarrassment.

I thought scullers strange when I first saw them while I was part of the rowing pack at the city club. My perception of scullers as a marginal subset of rowers—chess club, not varsity sports—didn't begin to change until after I started sculling and could appreciate how hard it was to get a twenty-six-foot boat down to the dock, out on the water, and back in one piece. I also came to admire scullers' self-discipline and passion for excellence. Sculling had started as Rowing Lite for me, with no intimation that it was to become much more. Buying my own boat was the beginning of an identity shift.

My boat arrived one beautiful, sunny, late-October day. I have a picture of it sitting in slings outside the boathouse, riggers on the ground beside it waiting to be attached. I am in the picture too, trying to appear casual, as if I don't have a premonition that this boat will become one of the loves of my life.

The club's dock was scheduled to come out for winter the following week. My plan was to get the boat ready for the next season and store it in the boathouse until then. The sun warmed me as I attached the riggers. When I finished, I stood back and admired the boat's whiteness shining in the bright autumn light. I looked out at the river, calm and quiet without its usual complement of buzzing motorboats, and couldn't resist going out, just once, not far, for a few minutes, to see how my new boat felt on the water.

Two rowing friends saw me off after coming down to the dock to admire the boat as if it were a new baby out for its first public pram ride. When I slipped my bare feet into the racing flats attached to the foot stretcher, I felt connected to the boat for the first time. Contact with the foot stretcher had previously been a matter of chance dependent on using heavy socks to pad my size-7 feet so they filled the size-12 shoes mounted in the club boats.

I pushed off the dock, came up the slide, and pulled my oars through the water. I felt glide so long and true that I could have been a hawk on a downward air current. I took more strokes, reveling in the feel of the boat under me. The dock had long disappeared from view, but I was enjoying myself too much to worry. And then the boat lurched to one side. I brought both oars perpendicular to the riggers, but the boat didn't balance. That was when I saw that the gate that kept my port oar rotating inside the oarlock without coming out had fallen off. I knew I was going over; it was just a question of when and where.

By carefully maneuvering the gateless oar, I was able to take short strokes toward the dock, but each bit of progress was a fight for balance. About one hundred feet from the dock, I capsized.

I remember feeling my arteries constrict as the water closed around my body. I remember thinking that if I didn't have a heart attack right then, I'd never have one. Sputtering, I surfaced and began treading water beside my boat. Without a gate to keep my port oar from sliding through the oarlock, it floated downriver with the current. I swam a few strokes in pursuit but realized the current was moving too fast for me to retrieve it. I breaststroked back to my boat and used the hull for flotation.

Without both oars to stabilize the boat, it was impossible to right it, let alone get back into it. Draped over the hull, I began kicking toward the dock. I kept gasping because the water was so cold, even with my upper torso out of it. And then I was lower in the water, not able to see over the hull as I had been before. Everything was quiet. My legs felt heavy. I stared at the boat thinking what a pretty white it was. A nap seemed like a good idea. I remember saying "help"—not shouting, not calling—more an admission to myself about what I needed. My capsize had attracted attention, and someone watching from the dock waded into the river, swam to where I was, and swam me and my boat to shore.

Although I didn't expect hypothermia to set in so quickly, the sleepiness I felt was an indicator of its arrival. The combination of cold water, my low mass, and the expenditure of effort all contributed to a truncated survival time for me.

I had been a timid sculler when I believed capsizing meant not being able to get back into the boat, but once I understood that capsizing also might not be survivable, that water temperature was determinative, I could feel fear slithering toward me and what I had begun to love: my boat, moving on the water, solitude. As frightened as I was, I was even more determined not to give in to fear. I knew that if I did, I would never go out again.

Hoping to appease the gods of fear, I vowed that I wouldn't go out in my single in early spring or late fall when the water was cold and potentially hypothermic. The following summer, I did whatever it took to get myself out on the river — bribing myself with food, shopping, reading, marshmallow chicks. I had no shame. Crossing some patches of water, I held my breath, and my hands tightened on the oars as I imagined monsters of the deep watching, waiting for me to fall in. To counter that, I'd conjure up a picture of my island. If I could reach its shelter, I would be safe, even if only for a few minutes.

At the island, my imagination, temporarily freed from dire thoughts, turned to inventing stories about pirates and people on the lam from life who inhabited the island. I listened to tree whispers for clues about their stories. Because I felt safe, for a time, I became a child—protected, unobserved—who played there. I'd come up the slide pretending I was a cheetah: silent, powerful. I talked to the ducks that detoured around my boat; it seemed the neighborly thing to do. I imbued heron sightings with meaning as if they were visitations from the spirit world bringing a message I was supposed to understand. For a long time, I never went beyond the island.

15
Women's Four

Shortly after the docks went in the next spring, while I was under my self-imposed interdict to not go out in my single until the water warmed up, I got a call from a club member trying to organize a women's four. The idea of rowing again interested me. My cautious sculling style wasn't much of a workout. Even though I could elevate my heart rate by just thinking about going out in my single, I was pretty much running the equivalent of a 20-minute mile when I was on the river. I thought rowing would provide more physical exertion, get me out on the water earlier, and maybe help my sculling technique.

Three of us showed up for the meeting, one rower and a coxswain shy of being able to go out in the club's only four-person shell. We all worked to recruit a fourth woman but only got qualified promises: "If I'm in town"; "If I can get a sitter"; "If I don't have aerobics." Once a week, I would tear out of work, drive 45 minutes to the boathouse in rush-hour traffic, change, and wait with the other two women until it was certain no one else was coming. After two weeks of this, a woman who had been in a boat only a few times, but was willing to show up on a regular basis, came and we had our women's four. We paid any high school student willing to learn to steer to be our coxswain.

Not one of us had rowed in college, let alone in high school, and we didn't have a coach, or even the possibility of a coach, so we became a boat of autodidacts, dealing with our most immediate and significant problems first: the boat rocking from side to side and our oars going into the water at different times. We all had theories about causes and solutions; every hypothesis was eligible for testing. Our women's four became a floating problem-solving group. We'd talk about what we thought we should do, reach consensus, do it, then hold another in-boat meeting to decide what we were going to do next.

One of the women in the boat was dating a club member who rowed in the men's four, so she was able to report on what the men did, which, it turned out, was whatever their coxswain/coach told them to do. They did not strive for consensus or drift into conversations about jobs, bosses, where they'd gone, where they wanted to go, what mattered to them. They did not stop rowing to watch sunsets or look at interesting cloud formations. But we also rowed in downpours and whitecaps and could carry the heavy wooden shell down to the dock by ourselves. We knew that all of this was noticed.

I have a picture of us rowing in our first race at the club's annual fall regatta. The oars on the port side of the boat are knifed in the water, three of us are at the catch, blades ready to pull through, and one of us is en route. Despite this poster display of bad technique, we found it exhilarating just being in the boat and racing.

That first year I rowed in the women's four I thought I knew what it must be like to be in a girl gang that was exceptionally democratic. We were all responsible for what happened in the boat. Out on the river in the boat, there were no male bosses demanding, needing, wanting us to be daughters, therapists, surrogate mothers. There were no husbands requiring attention, support, dinner; no children presenting as black holes of need. We were Toad and Mole messing about, sharing the river's rhythms, and treasuring a secret identity as athletes-in-progress. Pulling our oars through the water, feeling its resistance and overcoming it, we felt powerful.

We had only been out a few times in the women's four the following season when we heard about a three-mile citizens' boat race held around Memorial Day, known in local parlance as the "anything that can float" regatta. It sounded like fun, so we entered.

We were uncertain about the distance, three miles to the starting line and three miles back, but we had started saying "Why not?" more frequently than "Better not." We planned to meet at our boathouse an hour before the start so we would have enough time to row upriver at a leisurely pace. We had been waiting thirty minutes when we got a message that our stroke was stuck in a meeting and would have to join us at the starting line. Because it would take at least thirty minutes to row upriver if we wanted to get there before the start, we knew we had to launch right away. We talked our coxswain into rowing, assuring her that she wouldn't have to race, and arrived at the starting area with five minutes to spare.

The section of the river where boats had gathered for the start had a Dunkirk look. Everything in the county that could float was there, massed so tightly you could have crossed the river by stepping from craft to craft. There were sleek canoes paddled by kneeling pairs attired in spandex, pedal-powered rafts, rubber lifeboats, kayaks, and family canoes with mom and dad sitting in bow and stern, respectively, their tow-headed children arrayed between them. There were no other rowing shells.

We scanned the shoreline but didn't see our stroke. She saw us from the bridge where she had been standing looking for us and ran toward the boat just as we heard the announcement over the PA system that the race would begin in two minutes. We saw her hop into what I now remember as a washtub with a small motor that put-putted her toward us with maddening slowness. We heard the "get ready" command. The moment she got close enough to the boat to put her hand on the gunwale, the starting pistol went off. She swung herself into the boat as our coxswain catapulted into the cox seat. It was like watching aerialists perform.

As the boarding and catapulting was taking place, boats began rushing past us, tangling with our oars. Our coxswain tried to maneuver us out of the mass start, but it was impossible to get clear enough of the other boats in order to swing our twelve-foot oars back to the catch so we could grab water and move. Off starboard was a lawn chair float with an older couple in Bermuda shorts and matching fishing hats pedaling unconcernedly. An aluminum canoe with a family of five was off port. One swipe of our oars on either side would overturn them, spewing the occupants into the river and path of oncoming boats. Late-night dorm debates presenting ethical conundrums about whether a plummeting plane should crash into playing children or praying nuns came unbidden to mind. Finally, our coxswain shouted: "Just row. Hard. Now." I closed my eyes and obeyed. When I opened them, there was open water between us and the flotilla.

A year after that regatta, I stopped for an ice cream cone at a stand near the start of the race. As I was waiting in line, a man I had never seen before came up to me and said, "Aren't you one of those women that was in the rower last year?" My first thought was that we had taken out the elderly couple, and this was one of their children wanting to avenge his parents' dunking. "No," I said, recalling that some ethicists allowed lying for survival, and vowed to never appear anywhere upriver again without sunglasses and a big hat.

One of the many things I loved about rowing in that women's four was the sheer adventure of the thing, never knowing exactly what was going to happen. We always had a plan, but it was mostly used in the stories afterward for historical reference. Because almost nothing happened by design in the boat, we became world-class chaos-management specialists. Another thing I loved was the feeling that I wasn't alone, that no matter what happened, I didn't have to face it by myself; I could count on my crewmates. Years later, three of us from that crew would stand on the banks of a rapidly rising Charles River and decide we would race. There was no question but that I could trust them with my life, and they could trust me with theirs. We never got the chance to see what we could do because the race organizers canceled the regatta. While driving home, I wondered if what I had felt, a connection so strong it would hold love that transcended death, was what soldiers in combat felt. Or members of a good girl gang.

16
Fear Versus Desire

From the time he was a ten-week-old puppy, I knew that my male golden retriever had strong breed instincts. He never failed to track a plane flying over the house en route to the airport, somehow confident that if I'd uphold my responsibility and shoot it out of the sky, he could find it and bring it back to me. That was why I expected him to jump in and start swimming the first time he came upon an in-ground garden pool.

The water was shallow, about fourteen inches deep, but it was black, making it impossible to see the bottom. He ran to the edge of the pool and stopped. His older sister, whose breed instincts were more cat than dog, let alone retriever, jumped in. He paced and whined, went to the edge, lowered his chest; everything in his being was telling him to jump in, but he wouldn't leave the edge of the pool. It wasn't until I stood in the water, coaxing, reassuring him it was fun, everything would be all right, that he leapt toward my open arms and into the unknown.

In my battle between fear and desire, there were no arms to run toward, no promise of safety. I was on my own. I had to figure out a way for desire to prevail in order to continue going out in my single, and that meant finding some comfort in the helix of irrationality called sculling.

Although I had begun to love moving through the water in my boat and the solitude in which I did it, I was still afraid of capsizing. My descent into hypothermia had given me the perfect excuse to never go out: I might die. But I didn't want to use it. I wanted to continue sculling, just without risking death. My solution to this dilemma was a mental risk avoidance chart with hypothermia assigned top place on the list. A self-imposed prohibition to not go out in my single until late May or early June when the water temperature was in the survivable range reduced that risk. I also started going out in the early morning when there were fewer wakes. Most boats on the river then were parked for fishing and seemed happy to stay where they were. It made a difference to be on the water when I didn't have to assess wakes for their potential to capsize my boat.

I had learned to carry my boat on top of my head, something I was enormously proud of. At least I could look like a sculler on my way down to the dock. I had also learned that the most stable way to launch was bow out from the west side of the dock where, with a single hand push, my boat cleared the dock and I could begin rowing. It helped to have at least a couple of obstacles removed.

Even so, although I was connected to the boat at three points—hands, feet, and seat—I didn't always feel a secure attachment with my seat or oar handles. I squirmed on my seat at the dock and out on the river as well, searching for the elusive tongue-in-groove fit between it and my pelvic bones. My oar handles, although smaller in diameter than those of sweep oars, were still too big for me to comfortably maintain the correct grip: thumb over handle butt, fingers cradling the handle. When I wasn't squirming, I'd reposition my hands over the handles, hoping that I'd find a sweet spot so I could feel that the oars were an extension of my arms— wings to fly with. There were times, unexpected and fleeting, when I did.

I started to wonder if I had been wrong about why my sweet golden retriever puppy jumped into the water. Maybe it had little to do with me urging him to; maybe it had everything to do with him deciding he wanted to be in the water more than he wanted the safety of the known.

There was no river miracle. I continued to clench my oar handles and fight down panic when the boat rocked. But those moments, and that's all they were, when I became absorbed with the moving meditation of *catch, drive, release* and lost awareness of anything else occurred more and more.

17

Head of the Charles

More women joined the club and the following season the women's four expanded to an eight. We assumed that bigger would be better, faster, more fun. For the first time, we had a coach, a woman who had rowed in college and was looking for coaching experience as entrée to the competitive world of college coaching. We loved the idea of having a coach, reading into it the message that we had potential.

Our coach, who was about twenty years younger than most of us, was strong, smart, knew what she wanted, and didn't think it was selfish to pursue it. She could start a balky outboard and stand up in the aluminum launch to demonstrate a part of the stroke without going into the river. She had even trained her Labrador retriever, who accompanied her in the launch, to not jump into the river at will. We considered him an assistant coach with powers of discernment so great that when he barked, we assumed we were doing something wrong.

There were times when I would look over at her from the boat, her black Lab beside her, her hands tracing the path of a good catch in the air, and wonder if but for a couple of thousand different life circumstances, I could have been her. I wasn't alone. Our boat full of Ph.D.'s, engineers, and teachers all saw in her what we might have been and done if we had come to womanhood at a different time. And I understood a little of what my mother must have felt to have had a daughter for whom college was a given instead of a dream.

Rowing in the women's eight that first year was heady stuff. Just the fact that for the first time in the club's history there were enough women to fill sixty feet of boat made us feel that we were part of some noble experiment. The men in the club started referring to us as "the women," as in "the women are doing a 2500-meter piece tonight," "the women look fast." "The women," a class by ourselves.

The boat's roster depended on who showed up. Some evenings, only five women would show up for practice, and we'd end up going out in a four with one of the women coxing. For other practices, as many as ten women would show up, and delicate, indirect soundings would be taken before two women volunteered to leave. Sign-up sheets were tried, but children got sick, business travel intervened, and the myriad things done by women seemingly responsible for keeping the earth rotating took precedence. By midsummer, there was a core group of eight regulars who had gotten good at thrusting a chair between themselves and snarling demands. Stuck in a meeting at 5 p.m., half an hour before launch time, one woman excused herself to go to the ladies room and instead drove to the boathouse for practice. "They'll just think I was in there for a long time," she said. We all made mental notes to remember a visit to the ladies room as an escape tactic.

In August, our coach filled out an application to enter the Head of the Charles as a club eight but didn't tell anyone until she got notice we had been accepted. For club rowers like us, the Head of the Charles was where the gods of rowing walked among mortals. We wanted to be fast, exhibit flawless technique, and in a cherished fantasy, overhear onlookers commenting, "Who are those women? They're very good!" Although we weren't aware of it at the time, we wanted to be recognized as rowers, people who could move a boat, move on other boats, conquer, albeit with benevolence.

Even though we had raced three miles at our club regatta, we believed that the Head of the Charles three-mile-distance was different somehow, and if we didn't spend every day training all out for the race, we would fail our test of worthiness. So, in addition to the miles we rowed and raced during our on-the-water practices, we took a boat vow to do erg pieces as well.

A rowing ergometer, or erg, measures how much energy a rower is exerting against resistance. This indoor rowing machine has a sliding seat and a handle attached to a chain that moves a flywheel as you pull it toward your body. The harder you pull, the faster the flywheel moves. To a certain extent, the movement mimics rowing—you come up the slide, you go down the slide—but without sensory feedback or balance demands. Even though I can convince myself that running in single-digit temperatures with a biting wind will be just the kind of dermabrasion my skin craves, I have never been able to make myself believe that erging is anything but torture. If prayers can cancel time in Purgatory, time on the erg can erase years in Hell. And yet, I never missed one of the pre-Charles erg workouts. A vow is a vow.

A month before the race, I found a lump in my breast. Surgery as soon as possible was recommended and scheduled for the week before the Head of the Charles. I asked if I would be able to row the following week. "Doubtful," was the surgeon's assessment. I told him the surgery would have to wait until after the race.

An entourage accompanied us to Boston: club members, friends, husbands, relatives. We assembled at Magazine Beach, the staging area for the regatta, a dusty bank of the Charles River west of Boston University Bridge and within a short walk of MIT's campus. Row after row of boat trailers, long and high enough to accommodate stacks of rowing shells, flew school flags from their parapet-like upper reaches. These flags and adjacent canopies in school colors conveyed medieval fair to me. Rowers walked between the trailers in their team jackets, visiting friends and checking out the competition. We didn't have team jackets but used the sports attire parade to window-shop while waiting for the trailer with our boat on it to arrive, taking instantaneous polls on colors and lettering in anticipation of the day we might own such apparel.

We had heard that the Charles was a tough course with a 180-degree turn between start and finish and narrow passage under bridges. We had also heard stories about fights breaking out between rowers, with oars used as jousting lances, as shells sought to occupy the constricted space under bridges at the same time. When the trailer arrived, the club members who had accompanied us helped to reattach the riggers so we could get out on the river to familiarize ourselves with the race course.

There were glitches reassembling our eight. Compared with the other boats we saw coming off trailers, ours was ancient, or more euphemistically termed "vintage," and had quirks accompanying that nomenclature. But we had a crack pit crew. Mostly scientists and engineers, they were all world-class problem solvers. I grew to appreciate being part of a club with such a deep analytical bench because I began to learn from them that there were usually more options than helplessness in the face of adversity. When we proceeded to the dock for our practice row, there were about twenty people carrying the boat. I never felt its weight.

Race day was cold and sunny. I thought that our event, the women's club eight, meant we'd be competing with other rowing clubs like ours, enthusiastic amateurs. I learned, however, that in Head of the Charles terms, "club" pretty much means any crew that has not won a world championship in the year the regatta is held. That we were in over our heads competitively was emphasized for me when, huddled in the polar fleece jacket I wore over a polypropylene thermal shirt and a turtleneck, I watched the crew next to us strip to unitards, exposing bare skin to the chilly air as we waited to be called to the starting line.

There were forty boats in our event, and we were next to last to be called to the starting line, so I had time to sit in the starting area, look at the Boston skyline, and think about the lump in my breast. Living in the present had always been an abstract notion to me, something that sounded good but whose practice had eluded me, until now, when I realized I might not have much of a future. I looked out over the armada I was part of, felt cold air on my cheek, and cried, silently, happy to be where I was, wanting nothing else at that moment. Then we were called to the starting line by race traffic controllers, the aquatic equivalent of border collies in launches, and given commands: "half pressure," "full pressure in five," "you are across the starting line," "have a good day." I rowed with ferocity, determined that if this were to be my only Charles, I would hold nothing back.

Despite our passionate rowing, we came in near the bottom. We tangled oars with a boat under a bridge, and words were exchanged. Precisely: our honor student, angelic-faced, private Catholic girls school fifteen-year-old coxswain shouted at the coxswain of the other boat, loudly enough for the crowd gathered on the bridge to hear, "GET THE F**K AWAY FROM MY BOW."

The official race pictures I ordered were the next size down from wall panorama. My lump was benign.

18

Falling Out of the Boat

I continued to scull in the mornings the following season. On one of those mornings, while I waited for sun to burn through an unexpected fog on the river, another sculler arrived. We talked until the fog lifted, and then she suggested we set out together in our singles.

As soon as we turned our boats upriver, she pulled ahead but stopped several times for me to catch up. She had been to a sculling school in Florida over the winter and wanted to share a technique-improving drill she had learned there: sculling with square blades.

I had done this drill in an eight and a four, and it scared me to death in those wider, more stable shells. If not executed perfectly, the blade's edge clips the water, causing the boat to lurch to one side and potentially keep going. She demonstrated, stubbing her blade edge once but then quickly regaining control.

"This is a great drill for hand levels and balance," she said, urging me to try it.

I didn't, sure I'd capsize if I did. But with her as my escort, I grew daring and rowed past the invisible fence at the end of the island that I had never gone beyond. When we stopped for a water break, she told me she planned to scull another two miles and invited me along. I made something up about having to get back.

I should have been honest and told her that another two miles was not in my repertoire, that simply going past the island had been a huge psychological victory for me, but I didn't because that confession plus not even trying square blade rowing would have revealed that I was incompetent and pathetic. Scullers are supposed to be competent and tough. Especially tough. By the time I turned around, her boat had moved around a bend in the river and was out of sight.

Maybe it was the August sun beating down on me, warming my muscles. Maybe it was knowing I had broken out of my self-imprisonment without the gods in full thunderbolt-throwing pursuit. Maybe I wanted to prove to myself that I could be tough. I don't really know why I abandoned my cautious, tense sculling style and whaled my oars through the water. Or thought I had. I expected to hear a *whoosh* as my oars moved through the river. Instead, I fell out of the boat with a *plop*.

It happened in a heartbeat. One second I was catching hold of the river with my oars, and the next I was in the water. It felt like I had all the time in the world between my port blade coming out of the water high, the boat rolling to starboard, and me slipping into the river as smooth and easy as an oyster into a waiting mouth.

My first surprise was how unexpectedly pleasant the water felt. I was hot and sweaty; the river felt cool and soft. But I knew I couldn't stay in the middle of the river forever. I had to get back into the boat. The question was how, since all I had to work with was theory, having failed capsize re-entry at sculling school. The dock was two miles downriver, and I was a quarter of a mile from either riverbank; there was no way I'd be able to stand up to re-enter the boat. I reviewed my Capsizing 101 notes and recalled the coach saying that the most important thing in boat re-entry was holding the oars together in one hand and never letting go of them. I would do that.

One oar was at a steep, crazy angle from the boat. When I reached for it, the boat turtled, something I wasn't expecting and didn't know how to reverse. I tried pressing down on the near rigger to right the boat, but with no result. I then tried to pull the far rigger toward me but couldn't reach over the hull. Finally, I dived under the boat and pulled the far rigger through the water. The boat turned right-side up. Heartened by this success, I reached for the oars to draw them together, but one oar remained tantalizingly out of reach. Every time I lunged to grab it, it moved away from my hand. I tried again and again for what seemed liked hundreds of reaches and eventually grasped it. By this time, I was getting tired. I looked upriver to see if my companion might be returning, but it was just me and the river and the boat.

According to my Capsizing 101 notes, the next step was hoisting myself into the boat. Hoisting was the part I failed to execute at camp. It had been explained as placing the non-oar-holding hand on the deck of the boat, rising out of the water with a push, and swinging your butt on to the seat. In ballet, if you don't execute a step correctly, the instructor moves your body, arms, feet, into the right position. In sculling, words are used for teaching technique and their meaning comes in the same way as enlightenment, after years of meditation and miles of experience. I didn't have that kind of time to figure out how to get back into my boat. I wanted somebody there beside me right then, moving my body into the right position, or at least pasting footsteps and handprints on my boat for me to follow. But it was just me and the boat.

I pushed against the deck with my free hand, kicked underwater, and managed only to get high enough to smash my elbow on the metal of the slide track. Blood ran down my arm. I sank back into the water. On my next water vault, I achieved enough height to lay my upper torso across the track before I sank back into the water. I tried over and over, losing height with each jump. No matter what I did, I couldn't get enough height to swing my butt into the boat. The refreshing coolness I felt when I first slipped into the water was gone. Now the water felt cold as though it was hardening around me, encasing me in the river.

What I had feared most had happened, I couldn't get back into my boat. Magical thinking that I wouldn't fall out of my boat as long as I tightly controlled every motion, every breath, had blinded me to the reality I was in a craft designed for failure such as capsizes, and the sculling aphorism "there are two kinds of scullers: those in the water and those about to go into the water" is a succinct statement of truth. I would have laughed at the juxtaposition of my idea that I controlled the boat with the reality of me treading water beside it had I not been so focused on getting back into the boat. I made a mental note to myself: any fool can fall out of a scull; the trick is getting back in.

I looked around. A heron watched me from a snagged limb on the distant riverbank. I tilted my head back, took a deep

breath, drawing in the heady river brew of decay and regen-
eration. I heard the call of birds I could not see. I recalled those
moments in the boat when I had forgotten my fear and glided
through the water. I wanted to do that again. I treaded water
beside the boat, letting this longing gather force. Then I pliéd
under the water, jumped, hurled myself across the tracks, and
hauled my butt into the boat an inch at a time.

I felt lighter after my baptism, after losing the weight of
fear. I kept my feet on top of the shoes on the foot stretcher,
moving as lightly as a leaf on water. I floated like a tropical
fish, sleek and silvery and iridescent blue with black stripes
and eyelash-like gills, in a tank of my own devising. I heard
the water in the bottom of the boat slosh from bow to stern. I
laughed out loud.

19

Roaming

Because I was the only one at sculling school who couldn't get back into a capsized boat, I believed I'd never be able to. That deeply held conviction acted as a spell of sorts, controlling my every action, breath, and thought while I sculled. Because I believed I was a frog, I croaked. Or in my case, did nothing to jeopardize staying in the boat.

There are many ways to break a spell, e.g., burning a bay leaf at dawn, moving a salted lemon around your body, reciting the 37th Psalm, and it turns out, the highly recommended method of taking yourself to a body of water and jumping in. Although my re-entry after capsizing was ugly and arduous, it dispelled my conviction that it was impossible. I was now at liberty to move about the river.

I had been sculling in the mornings, waking to first light and on my way to the river soon after that. When I arrived at the boathouse, I pushed the barnlike bay doors open and set out slings before removing my oars from the rack where they were stored with other boat owners' oars. I could pair oars with scullers by the colors, patterns, and stripes painted on each blade like a coat-of-arms designed to stand out for quick recognition in battle. I carried my oars down to the dock and before climbing back up the hill to the boathouse, checked wind and current while observing the morning's activity on the river: a mother Canada goose with downy offspring who followed her from the dock into the water, a fishing boat parked by the rocky outcrop of land across the river.

I signed out in the spiral notebook kept on a shelf at the front of the boathouse in which scullers enter date, boat used, destination, time out, and time back. Destination is binary: upriver or downriver. At the beginning of the season, the notebook is fat with paper. By the end of the season, the book has been looted for bulletin-board notes. But nobody touches the pages with the accounting of who has gone where.

Those pages showed that the club's scullers roamed the river. Except for me. My destination was always the same: upriver. Even though I had gotten better at docking, could scull a straight course, and charm fear's moving head with the music of concentration, I followed the upriver trail from dock to island and beyond by default. I knew what to expect, which buoys I had to watch for. I didn't know what would happen if I left that groove of safety.

After signing out, I lowered my boat from its nest high in the boathouse heavens, pliéd under it to get the seat on my head, and walked down to the dock. There was nothing about this routine that I didn't love.

Although I continued to denote upriver as my destination, I wanted to be the kind of sculler who decided on a whim where to go, who took not just wind, current, and water level into consideration before choosing a destination but desire as

well. What did I want? What was I hungry for? Solace? Play?
Purpose? Even though I didn't know what would happen if I
deviated from my routine, I wanted to explore and see parts of
the river where I had never gone. This safety-versus-risk debate
might have gone unresolved in my head forever had not two
women in the club suggested that we go out together in our
singles. So one morning we set off downriver, their preference,
in our needle versions of the *Niña*, the *Pinta*, and the *Santa Maria*.

We had to pass under a bridge spanning the river. Rowing
under bridges reminded me of hiding under the dining room
table as a child when I wanted safety or peace or both. Traveling
under this bridge evoked that feeling, a good start for setting
off into the unknown. On the other side of the bridge, high cliffs
bracketed the river and water cascaded down rocks along the
way. I became a tourist, stopping frequently to take in the sights,
forgetting that I was someplace I had never been, captivated
by what I saw.

The other women I had set out with turned around to go
back not long after we launched. I elected to continue on by
myself. It meant I would be alone, which, at that moment, felt
more like joy that I had the river to myself than terror that I had
only myself to rely on.

The sun lasered through shirt, skin, muscle, heating my
bones. It was peaceful on the river: too late in the day for fishing boats, too early for jet skis. I played, approaching the catch
exponentially, trying to halve each advance, until I found myself
with torso pressed against bent legs, arms closer to the stern
than usual. Previously programmed alarms went off in my
head: *Danger! Resume usual position! Fast! Before it's too late!* I

ignored them, plunked my oars in the water, pushed back with my legs, and propelled my boat through the water. As soon as I had, I knew that this was connection, the Holy Grail of sculling that coaches talked about. It felt as though there was some divine current moving through me and the river at the same time as my boat moved through the water.

At sculling school, I had watched videotapes of scullers who, as the coaches pointed out, all had great connection. But I watched with no understanding of what that connection was. Words were used to describe it, which I translated into the segmented *armsbacklegs/ legsbackarms*. But as I discovered in my boat that morning, using words to describe connection was as inadequate as using them to convey what a warm spring night feels like or how blueberry pie tastes.

Now I understood viscerally that my concentration on segments of the stroke was tedious and limited. Sculling was not about freeze-framing a catch or recovery; it was about the cycle of moving the boat, the whole greater than the sum of the parts.

After that realization, I looked at the river differently, thought about its inexorability, its power: water flowed from melting snow and ice in the spring, gathering force as it joined with streams and creeks, carving banks, smoothing rocks, shaping everything in its path. It was indifferent to me, and I found that indifference comforting. My idea that the river and I were opponents in perpetual conflict now seemed silly. I laughed at the idea that I could mean anything to the river. I felt more relaxed, lighter in my boat. I could still sense when I was over deep water, but I began to experience fullness instead of terror.

Feeling a boat/body/water connection began to change how I moved in the boat. I became focused on moving the boat with grace and power and, at the same time, fusing the individual components of the stroke into a system to achieve that. I constantly assessed and tried to identify and fix misfiring parts. Physical and mental exhaustion competed.

I had watched Buddhist monks construct a sand mandala of compassion in a chapel at a local university. Many of the monks had been imprisoned and tortured, and as they worked with sand representing the colors of earth, water, fire, wind, and sky, they prayed for forgiveness for their captors. When the mandala was finished, the monks swept the sand into an urn and released it into the river.

I watched from the college dock as the monks upended the urn so that the river, an artery of the universe, could carry compassion and forgiveness throughout the cosmos. I added reverent to how I felt about this now holy water.

I was still in the eye of change though and hadn't registered this shift in consciousness until I arrived at the boathouse one morning and saw gray clouds pregnant with rain. The forecast was for showers, heavy at times, later in the day. To me, this meant I could go out and get back before it rained. I figured that the worst that could happen was that I'd get a little wet.

It turned out that later in the day came earlier than expected, and "showers, heavy at times" was accurate if you dropped the "at times." Sitting out there on the river, alone, in my boat, watching water cascade down the visor of my cap, I heard the Voice of Should tell me that rain was miserable and must be fled for shelter and dry clothes. But that voice was drowned out by the sound of rain on water, percussive and melodious at the same time. The rain struck the water hard enough for symphonic effect, creating a curtain of sound around me. There was no one else out there; I was alone. Except for water. Water everywhere. I could have been in a waterfall. Or a dream world.

Clara Pinkola Estes writes of the legend of the bone woman, an old woman living in the desert who sings over bleached dead bones she brings into her cave until the bones become a woman who jumps up, runs out of the cave, and into the desert. The river's song of softness and power, of change and renewal, was starting to knit me together—body and soul.

20

Bow

Every rowing season begins with hope and the best of intentions: the season will start after a winter of intense erging, the same eight people will row together all season, and our coach will transform us into a winning crew. I signed up again to row in the women's eight because spring is a season of epidemic optimism and because it meant I could get out on the water earlier than my self-imposed late May/early June sculling timeline. Mostly though because memories of the heady days of rowing in the club's first women's four were still very much with me.

Our coach had moved on to the collegiate rowing world after the Head of the Charles. We missed her but were happy her career was taking off. Her replacement had worked as an assistant coach with a local high school rowing program, wanted to advance to the collegiate ranks, and no doubt saw us as a resume essential in terms of responsibility: "*Handled every aspect of coaching women rowers at club level.*"

More women had joined the club, and at least twelve showed up consistently to go out in the eight. The club had bought a used eight for us to row, a second- or third-hand boat, or maybe even a clearing-out-the-boathouse model that had been rowed hard before it came to us, but because it was lighter than the heavyweight boat we had shared with the men, we didn't care about its provenance.

The boat and new coach weren't the only changes in our rowing lives: the coach assigned seat numbers, eliminating our previous system of delicate negotiation over seating preference ("If you mind rowing stroke, I'll do it"; "I'd rather row a starboard position"; or "I'll row bow this time, if you do it next time we go out"). My seat assignment that spring was bow.

Many of the rowers who signed up to go out in the eight that spring were alums of the boat that had gone to the Head of the Charles the previous October. Despite our pride in participating in that race, we knew we hadn't offered competition to any other boat in our event; we just weren't good enough to do that. But we wanted to be. We resolved to improve, race in another Charles, do better. We were grateful for any instruction, doing whatever we were told to do, determined to get good— not subjectively good (we had learned that was self-delusion), but passing-boats-and-winning good. We wondered how we could have believed that joy equaled excellence.

When asked what our goals were, we told our new coach we wanted to be better rowers, shorthand for competitive, and gave him carte blanche to make us a faster crew. Our focus went from having fun to improving. We no longer stopped to watch herons take flight or observe a spectacular sunset. We had seen rowers at the Charles move boats with power and speed. We believed if we trained harder, we could compete—maybe not win, but at least not be consigned to the bottom of the standings. It was no longer enough to be messing about in boats.

When I rowed in the women's four and then the eight, I never thought about which seat I occupied in the boat. I was one of a crew of kindred spirits; that was all that mattered to me. I didn't anticipate rowing bow would be any different from rowing any other position.

From my new seat assignment at the back of the boat, I could see who rolled up early for quick blade entry at the catch and who didn't. Who knifed the blade deep into the river rather than letting it find its true depth, somewhere around just-covered. Who dragged an oar across the water, sloughing speed off the run of the boat. Who skyed an oar, causing the boat to lurch to one side. I began editing the boat. When I saw 4-seat sky her blade, I compensated by lowering my hands. I did it instinctively at first. All for the good of the boat.

A set eight-oared shell, one that does not rock from side to side, achieves that set or balance because eight rowers, working as a unit, execute complex movements with little or no deviation. All eight oars go into the water at the same time, at the same depth, come out at the same time, and are carried over the water at the same level on the way to the catch. Set is the *sine qua non* of good rowing.

In my single, responsibility for correcting set errors is mine, as is responsibility for not making them in the first place. I know in an instant if my boat is unbalanced. I feel movement toward port or starboard before I see it, and in another instant make the required adjustment to restore balance. In the eight, there were so many set problems coming at me in bow: timing, bladework, hand heights, whatever havoc a breakaway slide rush could wreak—that my position was overrun. I was in perpetual compensation mode: bow as crisis management.

Bow is supposed to be the boat synthesizer, the synchronicity gear, the harmonizer. All possible in a set boat. But in a boat with chronic balance problems, the only thing I synchronized was my frustration. I was happy to contribute to the boat's run by meshing timing, but it seemed more and more that my sole role as bow was to serve relentless and impossible demands to balance a boat swinging from right to left like a pendulum gone mad. As my self-pity deepened, I began to think of myself as Martha tending to the needs of guests while her sister Mary sat at the feet of Jesus, unencumbered by duty. I thought I remembered Martha having a meltdown and yelling at Jesus to tell Mary she needed to start trucking plates into the kitchen. It wasn't until later that I remembered Jesus' response was that Martha had to figure out what was important to her and do it. Not blame Mary.

21

Seceding

All happy boats are alike: oars enter and leave the water at precisely the same time; the boat has swing, that ephemeral sense that it is flying, the crew is capable of maintaining high stroke ratings for as long as needed; and everyone feels powerful, confident, like the best corps de ballet in the universe. Every unhappy boat is unhappy in myriad ways, beginning when the boat is being carried to the dock and its weight falls on only a few shoulders. Once on the water, one side or the other fails to set the boat, and it repeatedly dips; oars enter or leave the water at different times. Love only works if it's a shared illusion.

The women's eight continued to be a source of seemingly insurmountable balance problems. Before practice, we'd discuss possible causes and potential fixes. But no matter what we tried, we couldn't set the boat for more than a few strokes at a time once all eight of us were rowing at a higher cadence than twenty-two strokes per minute. The problem could have even been an undetectable defect in the boat.

No matter what issues or troubles there were in my non-rowing life, I had always been able to depend on the fact that going out in the eight would consume those problems like a fire burning trash into ash. But now rowing had become a problem, another problem I couldn't solve.

After the boat had been stored for the winter, four of us, over dinners and breakfasts, discussed our unhappiness and frustration about rowing in the eight. We were convinced that because we had tried everything we knew and nothing had fixed the set problem, the only solution was going back to what had worked for us before and rowing as a four.

It never occurred to us that that forming a four would be seen as rejection by our friends and fellow club members. We had tried to solve the set problems in the eight, everyone had, and failed. We needed an alternative because rowing in an unset boat wasn't just making us crazy, it was making us want to give up rowing. We knew that the men in the club formed different boats every season. It seemed our only option. Our coxswain told us that the women who continued to row in the eight referred to us as the Jurassic Four. When we were in the boathouse at the same time as the women's eight, there was courtesy but little warmth.

In preparation for rowing together, the four of us went to a one-week rowing camp run by an ex-Olympian. Our plan was to have the coaches there watch us row together, tweak our technique for speed and power, and then we'd go back to our river and put it all together. That didn't happen. We were never boated together and I spent the week seated in bow behind two women who had never rowed. Because these women didn't have even basic skills, they were a black hole of instruction swallowing almost all available coaching time and depended on me to set the boat.

It happens, especially in clubs, that more experienced rowers sometimes row with novices. It is like being asked to dance at a family wedding by a dear relative notorious for foot-crunching. You do it. You accept graciously. You say positive and encouraging things. You keep in mind that someone put up with you while you were learning.

When I was first seated by the coaches behind the women who had never rowed, I thought I was taking a turn at giving to the sport. Still there at the end of the third day of camp, I went to one of the coaches and told her that I didn't mind taking a turn rowing behind people who had never rowed before but felt I wasn't getting the experience I had come to camp for. I asked to be moved to another seat or assigned to a different boat. I made it to 5-seat the next day but then was back in bow, same boat, no reason given, until camp ended.

During an off-water lecture at camp, I learned that having good technical skills and being the lightest rower in the boat is usually the basis for designation as bow. But a technical skill commendation wasn't enough to block the realization that my lighter weight would always consign me to bow as a rower. It also appeared that not only had I been assigned to a caste from which there was no escape, but one that also made me invisible to the coaches at this rowing camp. I'd row as hard and perfectly as I could during the day in the hope that when the coaches got together at night to discuss the next day's lineup, one of them would say, "She's not big, but she moves the boat well," and my audition would win me a seat in a different boat.

Everyone from the club but me had a great rowing experience at camp. One woman was chosen to row in the coach's boat at the head race on the last day. Another had been chosen for extensive one-on-one coaching and had been videotaped five times to everyone else's two times. They all seemed delighted by the experience and returned the following year. I did not.

After we got back from camp, I resumed trading bow duties with the other starboard in our four. Because we had a set boat, I don't remember much editing, just rowing my heart out, feeling that in this happy family, any seat in the boat was a fine place to be.

Our practices in the four were heavy on technique and power drills. We assumed a correlation between performing a drill well and winning races, wanting to believe that tediousness of repetition and exactitude would eventually transform us into rowers with speed, power, and grace. We did miles of drills.

Our drills began as soon as we pushed away from the dock. With the bow pair steadying the boat with their oars, the stern pair did a warmup drill, usually a pick drill that progressed in twenty-stroke increments from rowing with arms only, adding back, then half-slide, and finally full slide. After the stern pair rowed twenty strokes at full slide, bow pair did the same drill while stern pair steadied the boat. A sequence of drills followed, all done in pairs. Then the coach gave us more drills, but with all four of us rowing so he could see how well we set the boat. We turned around at the railroad bridge, about two miles above the dock, and rowed back to the dock at full power.

Our women's master four was accepted as an entry in the Charles that year. The weekend of the regatta, we arrived early enough on Saturday to go out for a practice. A hurricane had been making its way up the coast, but whether it would affect

Boston was still undetermined. The wind was already up on Saturday, and the whitecaps on the river made our practice feel more like ocean rowing.

I remember the sound of rain waking me several times that night as it pounded the window of my hotel room. When I set out the next morning for the regatta, there was only one lane that wasn't under water on Storrow Drive, my route to the regatta. I parked behind an MIT building and stepped into water almost even with my door sill when I got out of the car.

The race organizers hadn't decided whether to proceed with the regatta or not. We waited outside in the rain for the determination. There was no point trying to stay dry: the wind turned umbrellas inside out and Gore-Tex jackets exceeded waterproof limits in minutes. The four of us stood by the bank of the Charles watching rain fall in inches and the wind whip up surfable waves as we discussed whether to withdraw should the race be green-lighted. We could see how bad conditions were but were confident that we could row the course. We'd make adjustments, flip catch to lower wind resistance on the oar blades, do whatever it took to maintain connection, and use every fiber of our being to apply force when and where we needed it.

We agreed that it would be better to go out without our coxswain because no one wanted to explain to her mother that harm had come to her daughter in a boat race that was supposed to be about bragging rights. Before we could test ourselves and our boat in the storm, the organizers announced that the race had been canceled. I hydroplaned on the Massachusetts Turnpike all the way home.

To this day, the "hell and high water" Head of the Charles remains my favorite race I didn't row. Our decision to go out in close to hurricane conditions, with no coxswain, was rooted in our trust in one another and confidence in our rowing. That clarity produced a calm that contrasted with the wildness of the weather we had decided to take on. I still believe that we could have done exactly what we set out to do. We had become that kind of crew.

Because our race had been canceled, we were automatically entered in the next year's Head of the Charles. Before the race, we secured the services of a college coxswain who had once been a second-grade student in 2-seat's classroom.

On a crisp, sunny mid-October day, we waited with fourteen other women's master fours to be called to the starting line. From the moment our bow number was called to approach the starting line, we rowed with confidence and purpose. There was no ambivalence: we were doing this; we wanted to do this. We had arrived in Boston after a decision that estranged us from friends, a realization that we could trust one another with our lives, and a lot of hard work.

We attacked the course at full power, only varying that intensity by upping it in order to pass or hold off a boat that was gaining on us. Our coxswain navigated a course that he had plotted to keep us within bounds without wasting extra strokes. The first time we cleared a lane marker by inches, my eyes widened, but then I started to look forward to seeing how close he had decided to cut it. He coxed so brilliantly that when we passed the reviewing stand, the officials singled him out for it over the PA system.

We knew there were a lot of fast boats in our category, boats from all over the country, so we didn't expect to post the fastest time for rowing the three-mile course. Knowing that we had given it our all and rowed well was winning for us. I remember rowing back to the dock after we finished, spent but calm, our harmony and cohesion in sync with the river's flow. We placed 11th out of 14 boats officially, but from the picture taken after the race, you would have thought you were looking at the winning crew.

22

Leaving

After the next rowing season began, one of the women in our four had to travel for work more than she had anticipated, and we were usually short one rower. The women's eight had trouble getting enough women to show up for practice. Light on rowers, both crews drifted together to form one crew, and soon I was going out in the women's eight.

Practice was scheduled for 5:30 p.m. The boathouse was a forty-five to fifty-minute drive from work during rush hour, and it took me an extra fifteen minutes to walk to my parking lot to retrieve my car. Traffic varied from creep-and-crawl to gridlock. Every flash of brake lights triggered alternative route planning. When I arrived at the boathouse following this traffic induced high stress warm-up, I changed into my rowing clothes and then waited to see if we had enough women to go out and whether our coxswain had shown up. If we were carrying the eight out of the boathouse by 5:45 p.m., we were speeding along.

Once we got the boat to the dock, we'd spend at least ten minutes there adjusting foot stretchers and struggling to hand loosen rusted nuts that eventually required a trip to the boathouse for the toolbox. When we were finally away from the dock, we stopped after our warm-up drill while the coxswain and our coach discussed what we should do for the rest of the practice. During that discussion, I'd look at the riverbank from my seat in the eight and wonder how far upriver I'd be by now if I were in my single. Eventually, the discussion would end, and we'd start rowing by pairs, giving me more time to fantasize about being in a single as I sat balancing the boat, waiting for my turn to do the drill. All eight rowed continuously for only about twenty-five minutes before we reached our turnaround point and headed back to the dock. I estimated that my total time rowing was forty minutes, and that was if I had to take a lot of strokes as bow to line up the boat. Yes, I was back at bow. If only there had been a mournful, twangy country western song full of pithy truths that I could have hummed while I rowed.

I'd arrive home around 8 p.m., hungry, frustrated, and angry that I had spent more time getting to and from the boat than rowing in it. I started to resent the amount of time that rowing took. I rehearsed excuses for skipping practice but never used them. Duty kept me showing up.

Then one day at practice while I was tying in, I looked at my size-seven feet in the size-twelve sneakers on the foot stretcher, the space around me that I didn't begin to fill, the twelve-foot oar whose thick handle I couldn't rotate with just my fingers, and knew that the joy I had once felt rowing had been slowly eclipsed by a quiet, complicated, but profound love of sculling.

Still, I piled as much mental furniture as I could outside that realization's door. I tried ignoring the clamor of my heart telling me it was time to go. I had loved rowing with the happily ever-after conviction that we would be soulmates for life. Even the thought of leaving felt like a betrayal, a divorce, not a dramatic one in which crockery is satisfyingly and therapeutically hurled, but a miserable one in which the ripping asunder is a slow, relentless tear.

There was also fear in my realization. No more would I have the comfort of other oars to pull through rough water, the luxury of a coxswain's navigation, the strength of other shoulders to carry the boat. In my single, I was on my own, facing whatever happened on the water by myself. But I knew I had already spent too much of my life shortening my stroke, slowing my catch, trying to fit places where I did not. And deciding based on duty and fear, not love.

Sculling had begun to change me in different ways, one of them being my relationship with fear. My heart rate still went into fight-or-flight territory when I went out in my single, but I now anticipated that would happen and kept going, not because I was brave or courageous, but because I had become accustomed to fear as a constant companion. I stopped thinking about fear as something to be conquered, foot-on-the-neck vanquished, and started to think about my relationship with fear; we did spend a lot of time together, after all. I decided that if fear wanted to ride with me when I went out in my single, I wouldn't object as long as it was understood that staying dry depended on me. I hoped that Amelia Earhart was right about fear leading "to the place where you store your courage."

I still had *"Uh oh; I can't do this"* moments, and probably always would, so a truce with fear about our respective roles in the boat made sense to me. I even fantasized chummy conversations:

> Me: *Whoa, do you see that wake?*

> Fear: *You're still right-side up, chica; keep going.*

I didn't know if this détente would morph into collaboration; all I wanted was a way to be out there on the river in my boat, thinking my thoughts, sculling my stroke, setting my own course.

Rowing had given me back my physical self, reunited me with the child who loved moving, rhythm, glide. I thought I glimpsed her sculling close to the riverbank, singing a song whose words I couldn't quite make out while I was sightseeing in bow. I understood that I was sacrificing the stability, fellowship, and safety that rowing offered, but something was telling me it was time to light out for the territory.

I finished the season, but mostly it was a farewell tour: me gathering memories with each catch.

23

Competing

It is two hours past sunrise as I push off from the dock in my scull. Mist sleeps along the riverbanks. I head into it, breathing deeply, taking the mist inside me, holding it there, believing that when I exhale, I will be changed in some profound way.

As I approach the stone railroad bridge above the island, I hear the whistle of an approaching train and race to get there. I want to be under the bridge when the train clatters over the tracks above so that I can take in the sounds of engine, wheels, and whistle, and play a locomotion symphony in my head as I sit in my boat. I stay below the bridge until the caboose passes. Morning light, pale and clear, filters through the canopy of trees on the shore and spills into the river. When I squint, I see pools of diamonds sparkling on the water.

On my way back from the bridge, I sing, "Beyond the blue horizon waits a beautiful day..." At the island, I pull up to a dead tree limb protruding into the river and take a water break. I keep these branch ghosts company because they once let me escape their snare when I came upon them unaware. I deserved entanglement but received mercy instead. I start my favorite drill, no-slide sculling. I am mid-island when a single approaches. I hope the sculler and I will just nod to each other as he races by, but he stops, wants to talk, asks if I'll race him back to the dock. I demur.

"I'm working on technique; I'm not advanced enough to race," I say.

"Competition is the best method to improve technique. You'll never get good if you don't race," he says. "There's a race this weekend sponsored by a local club. It's always fun; you should go."

I know he is right. He is an excellent sculler and teacher, but I also know I won't go. I promise him I'll think about it. Frustrated by my intractability, he pulses past. I try to go back to the place where I had been in my mind, but it is gone.

*   *   *

Competition is the rule in sculling, just as it is in rowing. As with all physical endeavors, the assumption is that you scull for cardio fitness, muscle development, weight loss. Competition is part of that package, a way to keep score by measuring your ability against others. Win, and you never have to ask yourself "Why do I do this?" But I have never been good enough at anything for performance to be purpose, winning to justify doing.

When asked if I race, I almost growl my denial, angry that competing could be thought the only justification for the inexplicable. I am a mother bear defending tender purposelessness. Yet there are contradictions nibbling at my non-competition avowal. I distinguish racing in a shell from competing in my single because rowing in a four or an eight is about being with friends, and more than my effort is involved. Racing in a shell,

I've experienced the chant of charging oars, bodies swinging to the rhythm of that work—the power of battle cruising. But there have been times when I have wanted to race in my single.

At the club's annual regatta, the first races belonged to the scullers. I'd watch scullers, whom I had greeted and been greeted by as we glided past one another on perfect summer mornings, mass under the bridge by the boathouse for the start of their events. In the autumn light, through dispersing fog, the wing-shaped outline of those sculls brought to mind fighter planes named for raptors, thunderbolts, and sabres. I wanted to be with them, to be out there on the water, a sculler moving to the rhythm of blades and boat and water. I wanted to cross the starting line and hear the referee identify me by name and club, proof that I was a part of the squad. But I never entered. I knew that the entrants were competitive scullers. Not only wasn't I good enough to offer competition, I didn't want to defeat anyone. I just wanted to proclaim that I was one of them—*Je suis une rameuse:* I am a sculler.

24

Return to Sculling School

After experiencing that elusive boat/body/water connection where boundaries disappeared, I wanted to be able to re-create that feeling with every stroke I took. I knew doing that required good, probably superb, technique—something I didn't have and maybe never would. My form had improved, but I still expected my obituary to include a list of my technique flaws, starting with, "She was a kind person but known to rush her slide," and continuing on.

Among my many technique sins was an inability to get my oars off the water during the recovery. Instead of traveling silently above the water, my blades slapped the river. That bothered me because I liked to key in to the sounds of the boat. The click of oars beginning to turn in the oarlocks was my aural cue to catch, the whirr of my seat coming up the slide told me how fast my recovery was, and the plop of oars into the river retrieved my water connection. The sound of my oars dragging across the water not only interfered with that feedback, but was a constant rebuke that I was not holding up my end of the boat/sculler relationship.

I knew how I had acquired this problem—that was no mystery. In doing everything I could think of to stay in the boat when I started sculling, I had repurposed my oars to act as training wheels. But now I wanted to ride without that external stability. I wasn't confident that I could balance the boat without the prop I had relied on for so long, but I knew I had to try. Glide depended on not dragging my oars on the water.

I practiced drills with such focus that I frequently lost all sense of where I was until I'd just miss hitting a buoy. Normally, coming within striking distance of a buoy would have signaled failure and engendered self-reproach, but now, if nothing untoward happened to my boat, I didn't care.

Do I know you? I should have asked this strange woman who was suddenly indifferent to the prospect of a buoy collision. It would turn out that I did know her, but from a long time ago.

I read everything I could find on sculling technique. One Olympic coach suggested coming up the slide like a cat stalking a bird. I couldn't resist: I pretended I was a fluffy white Persian, a regal Abyssinian, a Siamese. I also pretended that I was the bird, an unsuspecting bluebird looking for worms, or a robin waiting for a turn at a feeder. But I had to imagine the bird flying away at the last possible moment.

Despite my nonpredatory cat practice, I still dragged my oars. When one of the women scullers in the club came back from a week at a sculling camp cured of blade dragging, I decided it was time to go back to school in search of improved technique. Maybe a fantasy of discovering hidden potential contributed to my decision as well.

I returned to the school at which I had matriculated as a nascent sculler. This time, driving for a distance down a dirt road didn't faze me, nor did the musty room or the capsize exercise. I knew what to expect. I could follow the dockside instruction; it wasn't a blur of information filtered through fear as it had been the first time. Skill level still determined lake location for on-water instruction. I wasn't grouped with the elite scullers at the end of the lake, but I didn't get assigned to the neophyte group kept close to the dock either. Middle of the lake was my classroom. I practiced drills, reviewed notes from videotape comments, and never missed going out for the discretionary afternoon session. When the last-day race came around, I felt ready to demonstrate the progress I believed I had made.

The race had a legend: a young sculler had thrown a dead fish into the boat of his nearest competition one year and surprised the other sculler into capsizing. Stories about money and jobs offered to coaches to influence the race's outcome were also told. Although the coaches mentioned that participation in the race was voluntary, that part was minimized while camp tradition and fun was emphasized. The task the coaches seemingly set for themselves in handicapping the race was to have the boats converge in an hourglass-shaped cinch in the middle of the lake that restricted passage to no more than three boats at a time.

The race was an exercise in truth because it wasn't until you were called to the starting line that you knew where the coaches ranked you. The boats deemed slowest started first. Until then, you were allowed to believe that the "betters" and "goods" doled out to you when observed meant something more than "Good job staying in the boat."

I knew the winner would be the kid we called "Harvard" because rowing there some day was the focus of his sixteen-year-old life. But I thought my improved technique would guarantee a solid middle-of-the-pack finish, with extra credit for style.

The coaches lined us up at the end of the lake for the start. A woman who had capsized so often that she had taken to wearing her bathing suit in the boat was the first called to the starting line. I watched her lurch from side to side as she sculled, wondering if she could stay in her boat for the two miles to the finish line.

After the coaches had called about half of the men in the next group, they called me. I was surprised and pleased that I was starting so late in the pack. My heart was pounding as I paddled up to the start. I heard "Go" and started sculling at full pressure, determined to justify my placement. I concentrated on form: fast hands, quick catch, strong leg drive. I was a swan gliding swiftly and powerfully over the water. Until I got to the cinch in the lake.

To avoid the traffic jam caused by the narrowed passage, I planned to hug the shoreline. I was headed there when the man who never looked where he was going the entire week rowed straight toward me. I yelled to warn him I was there, but he kept coming. I turned hard to starboard to avoid the collision. Oblivious to the barely avoided crash, he rowed past me.

The turn had altered my course, so I had to maneuver my boat to line it up for shore-skimming again. I had just picked up speed when another sculler entered the channel and headed toward me. I yelled his name. He looked right at me but did not alter his course. I yelled louder but got no response. When his boat was only inches away, I steeled myself for impact. He barely missed my boat but hit my oar. I thought I was going to capsize but managed to stay in the boat and finish the race. The only person I finished ahead of was the woman who had never sculled before.

It seemed I was more terrible than I thought. I felt as flattened as Wile E. Coyote on some desert canyon floor as the Road Runner beeped by. Maybe I wasn't a sculler; maybe I was just someone with a rich fantasy life.

There was one person that year who chose not to participate in the race, a fourteen-year-old who was there with her father. She was a strong, graceful sculler, someone who caught your eye when she was on the water—her movement was beautiful, rhythmic, mesmerizing. She was a sure bet to be among the top finishers and maybe was even capable of beating "Harvard." When I heard that she wasn't going to compete, I wondered how she could turn her back on almost certain victory. At the last practice, I asked her why she decided not to race. She told me she didn't enjoy competing. Although she sometimes raced in a four, she considered that to be more about rowing with her friends than competing. I admired how comfortable she was with who she was and what she wanted, and I envied it a little as well.

The week's instruction officially ended at noon and most people packed up and left before 11 a.m. I would have done that too, but there was something I wanted to do first. I went down to the boathouse and took out #12, the boat that had been assigned to me for the week. The dock was deserted as I pushed off and paddled lightly on the glassy lake. My breathing slowed; the sun warmed my arms and legs. I sat straighter, paying attention to form. "*Whoosh*," I repeated to cue myself for fast hands away; "*kaplunk*," I said to remind myself to not hesitate at the catch. I was a swan again, a white swan with a proud neck who moved like Pavlova or Makarova. When I arrived at the other end of the lake, I used the splash box for a pillow and dangled my feet in the water. The water was cool; the sun warmed my face. I looked up at the sky and watched drifting clouds. Time passed. I lost all sense of earthly orientation. I was at peace. I could go back.

25

Tempest

I had gone to sculling school in search of the perfect stroke. My quest had been unsuccessful, but I had learned to spin the boat, back it by reversing the blades and moving them toward the bow, and stop fast by using my oars as emergency brakes. Competencies so small, so basic, that they shouldn't have mattered. But they did. Knowing how to stop, turn, and maneuver the boat helped me feel confident. I didn't have to choose a spot on the river with a wide turning radius; I could turn anywhere. I didn't have to claw at the water with one oar and will the boat to turn faster when I heard the approach of a motorboat and its accompanying wake. It pleased me to be able to come to a quick stop when I needed to, much the same way I had liked shaving skating-rink ice with my T-stop. I felt more in control. An illusion, but one I was happy to have.

I buried my disappointment over my poor performance in the last-day race in each revision of the event I told. By winter, it had become a funny story. And despite my F in racing, I knew my sculling technique had improved.

Part of me still believed magic could be learned if I found the right teacher. When I found out that a coach acclaimed for his knowledge of moving boats would teach at the same sculling school for a few weeks the following year, I re-upped.

The coach's approach was fluidity: boat, body, water working together in a cycle. During the twice-a-day videotaping sessions on the water, he'd say something to me like "roll up earlier," watch me struggle to comply but say nothing until I had succeeded one time before giving me a "good; keep doing that," and motoring off to coach the next sculler. His refusal to mollycoddle or sugarcoat gave me hope that I could learn if I worked hard. That was important to me because no discernible talent for sculling had emerged, and hard work was all I had to offer. The tenets of his sculling canon—good technique, discipline, effort—made sense to me. I worked hard all week, doing drills from one end of the lake to the other trying to achieve rhythm, power, fluidity.

When another coach told me that two things were essential for lightweight scullers: perfect technique and being tough as nails, I took the advice to heart. When I wasn't working on technique, I channeled my inner Spartan warrior. I almost didn't sign up for the end-of-session race, but that year I was following these rules for life: show up, pay attention, tell the truth. "Showing up" got me to the starting line.

While I sculled as though my oars were calligraphy brushes—and sculling a visual art—everyone else hammered the water. I didn't come in last, but I was at the slow end of the time curve. Walking toward the dining hall for breakfast with the seventy-something-year-old man who had come in last for the past five years and expected to continue doing that, I confessed discouragement, the theme of which was I had done everything right, but it hadn't translated into speed.

He listened, gave no credence to my fear of taking last place from him, and said, "You'll get faster. Keep working at it." He told me that he looked at coming in last as an opportunity for graceful letting go of the desire to win. I admired his acceptance, the peace he had made with what he could do. But graceful letting go sounded to me like something else to practice that I no doubt would fail at.

I knew what I had to do. I'd go out one last time before driving home to remind myself what I loved about sculling. When I got down to the dock and saw the wind-whipped water, I considered not going out. But after observing the wind on the lake during the week, I believed that the far side, which I couldn't see from where I stood, would be sheltered from the wind. It wasn't.

I recalled Sylvia Townsend Warner's observation that "When you are down, everything falls on you" as I replayed the last-day race in my head. Blame and shame poured down on me. I thought I had made progress, had even gotten a "good catch" at a videotape session. Yet I was almost alone on the water when I finished the race. Everyone else had docked and gone to breakfast. Had I been deluding myself by believing that I could ever be a strong and graceful sculler? Was I an exception to the work-harder, get-better rule? And now I was on a choppy lake in a racing scull being tossed in troughs formed by swells. The only thing I was good at, it seemed, was ignoring reality.

I had to keep telling myself not to tighten my grip on the oar handles as the force of the waves hit them. *You cannot control the water*, I told myself. *All you can do is make sure your blades go in, through, and out.*

There was no calm water anywhere on that lake. I hugged the shoreline, risking collision with rocks and tree limbs, looking for some respite, but the wind was so stiff and multidirectional that even the shallower water offered no shelter. Exhausted and scared, I was ready to weep by the time I got to the other end of the lake. I didn't think I was going to make it back. I barely had the mental strength to resist taking my hands off the oars and surrendering to what I believed was inevitable: capsize and drowning. I had watched for another boat, hoping the sight of one would convince me that my fears were exaggerated, but there was no one else out on the water.

My racing boat wasn't made for these conditions, and I suspected, but did not want to verify, that my bow was under water at times. As the text under an illustration of a submerged bow in one of my sculling books said, "Only a very experienced sculler is able to handle a broaching bow without capsizing." Lacking that essential depth of experience, I wondered not if I'd capsize, but when. Then anger welled up from somewhere, anger at myself for going out, anger at the water for its rough treatment of my boat, anger over feeling helpless, powerless. An army of anger rose up and came to my aid. From someplace deep within me, I heard myself say, *I will not yield*. I looked around to see who had said that, I wanted to meet her but to do that I'd have to get back.

I breathed deeply before I turned around, swallowing panic as the water sucked at my blades, trying to pull them down to the bottom of the lake. The boat rocked in the whitecaps, and I lost half of each turn to the wind. It took pure will to turn, but I got my bow headed toward home.

I forced myself to think of nothing but *blades in, through, out*. I repeated this sequence mantra-like, hoping that the words would settle, maybe even weaken, my incipient panic. I jettisoned technique and shortened my stroke: *in, through, out*. I began to talk to the boat: "You can do this; you're a tough boat. We're almost there. Keep going. A little more."

When I passed through the narrow part of the lake, I felt that I was home, which for a sculler is a dock. I wasn't. I couldn't even see the dock from where I was, but it didn't matter. I knew I had passed through the worst of it.

After I got back to the dock and returned the boat to its rack, I ran to my room, collected my gear, and drove home. I didn't tell anyone what happened because for years I thought it was confirmation that I wasn't a good sculler, there would be no "someday" when I would be able to glide gracefully across water. I should have been more realistic about my limits, but acknowledgement and acceptance of limits is the gift of the secure, the proven.

I was certain that any other sculler would have rowed through the roiled water without even registering difficulty. I spent the rest of the summer seeking the solace of solitude on the river, accepting that I wasn't good, had barely adequate technique, would never be fast, and should be grateful I could stay upright in the boat at all. I found myself going out on the river more often. I had nothing to lose, nothing to prove. And with that out of the way, I discovered that I wanted to be on the river simply to be there, to say hello to the duck who guarded her flock by squawking whenever motorboats got too close to the rock where she sat, to race for the bridge when I heard the train whistle, to hear the *whirr* of my seat as I moved up the slide and the *plop* of my oars as they went into the water.

Years later, I re-evaluated what had happened during my post-graduate sculling school races. To avoid collisions with hell-bent boats violating every rule of navigation written, I stopped racing. That meant I lost time. It didn't mean I was terrible, just crash-averse. As for my perilous voyage in rough water, figuring out what I had to do to have a shot at surviving and not jumping into the riptide of panic was what had gotten me back with the boat intact. I didn't have medals or trophies, probably never would, but that mattered less and less as I reconnected mind, body, and soul in my boat, on the river.

26

Rowing to Eden

Sculling involves constantly assessing risk. *Is the water too cold to survive capsizing? Will a two-foot increase in the river level create turbulence? What is the wind speed? Is there a possibility of thunderstorms in the forecast?* It is easy to be seduced by rationalizations minimizing risk when faced with high water, fog, cold, wind: you tell yourself that you've survived worse, it's not so bad, you can compensate, you know what you are doing. Cue the siren song of adventure music, and you imagine feats of derring-do that will become stories proving you are tough, maybe invincible. Even more dangerous, though, is growing accustomed to water in its placid state and assuming that a calm surface denotes lack of power.

It takes seeing a raging river, or reading about a championship-caliber sculler who never returns from a swollen river, to understand that you are nothing against that power, that you and your preposterously skinny, fragile boat can be flicked away as easily as a leaf in a gale. Your safe passage depends on the kindness of water.

Sometimes, though, it happens that you set out in perfect conditions, a sunny day with not a cloud in the sky, only a light breeze livening the water, and a storm comes up with no warning, as if it has the wrong address to deliver its tempest to. The only thing to do then is seek shelter. If you can find any.

One summer, when the solace of the river had become essential for me, I found it impossible, even very early in the morning, to find peace there. Kamikaze bass boats using the river as a speed track created eternal wakes and terror, forcing me to assess whether the Darth Vader-helmeted driver coming straight toward me saw me and could or would change course, or if I should dive overboard immediately in an attempt to save myself. Other motorboats with engines the size of man-cave refrigerators created surfable wakes. As I rocked in my boat, I mentally raised my fist to the heavens, since I couldn't take my hands off my oars without capsizing, and vowed that someday I would find unroiled water.

Not long after that vow, I heard about a writing retreat on a motorboat-free Adirondack lake. The website mentioned a variety of boats available to participants, but sculls weren't on the list. I called to ask if they were part of the fleet.

"Do you have sculls?"

"What's a scull?"

I described it.

"No, nothing like that. Sounds interesting, though."

"Could I bring mine?"

"Sure. Things are very relaxed here."

I imagined sculling myself into a zen state before writing workshops, then heading for a cove in my boat in the afternoon, the water gently rocking me to sleep after I had composed haikus about clouds. I signed up. Only after I had sent my deposit did I think about how I'd get my boat there.

My boat's hull is made of the same composite as the wings of some airplanes, material that's water-slicing stiff but too fragile to survive falling off the roof of a car, which is how I would have to transport my boat to what I called "Paradise Lake." The practical exigencies of driving my scull from the boathouse to the lake were daunting. Not only didn't I have a boat carrier, I didn't even have a roof rack to attach a carrier to. Even more important, I had never transported my boat, wasn't brave, and hated risk.

My boat leads a cloistered life, only venturing from the boathouse to go out on the river and then returning to its cradle and space in the rafters after being lovingly washed and wiped dry with a baby soft towel. Nothing could hurt it in its eyrie; so many dire things could happen if it were to leave there.

Although the prospect of transporting my boat terrified me, I knew this: I had a choice between pursuing a dream or living with regret. I had lived with regret; it felt like cold fog seeping into my soul, draining warmth, blocking light. I chose terror. Who wouldn't?

A sculling friend lent me a boat carrier and I bought a roof rack after some internet research. Japanese manufacturer, Swedish manufacturer—*what's the difference?* I thought. I should have known after owning a Volvo and a Honda that there is a difference: Swedish engineering is complicated.

The roof rack from the Swedish company was delivered to my door just days after I had ordered it, a glad-to-be-an-American-in-the-21st-century moment. Heartened by the statement on the instruction sheet that no tools were required, I began assembly in my driveway over a three-day period, in heat and humidity so high that my contact lenses fogged. The instructions were in pictograms, which required an advanced degree in engineering, a lifetime of experience using tools, and fluency in hieroglyphics to interpret. None of which I had.

I'd get one bracket together, but before I could celebrate, it would fall off. And it had taken me two hours to get to that point. If I had been transporting anything other than my scull, I might have used a couple of rolls of duct tape to attach the rack. But I knew that the boat staying in the carrier depended on the rack staying on the car. When I began to entertain the notion that my failure might have been for the best, that maybe the carrier had to be attached to an *unassembled* rack, I recognized my Dr. Pangloss gene surfacing, which usually means incipient disaster, so I called one of my sculling friends for a pre-emptive intervention.

"No," he told me, "the rack has to go on first." And fortunately for me, he offered to help.

Two hours later, the racks were on, and I felt much better about my inability to get the job done by myself. I was an English major. Crows have greater tool ability than English majors. And there was no way I could have gotten the rack on by myself. Nowhere did the instructions mention that you need at least two people for installation because when you tighten one side, the other comes off without a second person to hold the bracket in place. Attaching the boat carrier to the roof rack was the easy part; it took five minutes once the rack was in place.

I liked having a five-foot steel bar with slings on the top of my car. The steel bar supporting the boat sling was a light gunmetal color that combined function and beauty. A bird-like whistling sound accompanied me whenever I drove. I didn't have to remember landmarks to find my car in parking lots. And it was changing my idea of who I was: a woman pursuing a dream. My anxiety about transporting my scull gave way to a can-do feeling that lasted until an image of me weeping by the side of the road, my boat shattered around me, displaced it. Reminding myself that I had decided to live with terror rather than cold regret restored some equanimity.

The Friday before I left for Paradise Lake, I went to the river to scull and saw a car at the boathouse with the same boat carrier and roof rack I had. I wanted it to be a message from the gods that portents were good for my journey. The carrier belonged to a smallish woman in her late twenties who could not answer my questions about how she had lifted her boat onto the carrier or tied it down because someone always did it for her. I went instant Eeyore, but my wallowing in self-pity changed to quivering when she told me that transporting a scull is "really, really scary." Her only advice: "Make sure everything is strapped down tightly."

I had three straps, one each for bow, middle, and stern, but my fear was now far beyond three-strap terror. I decided to buy at least another three straps, industrial strength, in the belief that lashing was my only hope. When I told the salesman I would be transporting a single scull and started to explain what that was, he stopped me, introduced himself as a rowing coach, and asked to see my car and carrier. After checking both, he said, "You're good. Transport should be a piece of cake."

I took heart from his assessment until I recalled that rowing coaches shimmy tractor-trailer-size carriers, boathouses on wheels loaded with eights and fours, into spaces that seem as narrow as a french fry.

My third opinion came from a coach who had transported her boat numerous times and was at the river that Saturday giving a sculling clinic. I launched to get to the coaching site just in time for the Grand Prix start of one of the almost-weekly bass fishing contests on the river. I rocked and rolled in motorboat wakes the entire time. My crazy decision to take my boat to a lake that banned motorboats seemed like sanity after that.

She told me I needed a boat cover to prevent pebbles kicked up by trucks from damaging the finish. I didn't have a boat cover.

"Take the riggers off to prevent the nuts and screws from getting loosened by the wind."

I hadn't planned to.

"Take your shoes out, or bugs will fly in there, creating a squishy, dead-insect insole."

I had planned to leave them in the boat.

"Bungee cords, not straps, because bungee cords will allow the hull to flex, desirable for carbon fiber."

After spending an additional one hundred and thirty dollars panic shopping, I thought I was ready. I worked from three lists and kept adding items. I panicked with geyser-like regularity. I half hoped that some *deus ex machina* would cancel the writing workshop. Living with terror was exhausting. Routine was so comforting, so like the pillow I wanted to rest my head on before falling into prolonged sleep.

I arrived at the boathouse just as my friends who had volunteered to help me drove up. Their good-heartedness meant the world to me. I had heard Ted Nash, the legendary rowing coach, give a talk about rowing in which he said that if you think the only benefit of boat club membership is access to boats, you are cheating yourself because the most significant benefit is the people in the club. I recalled his words as we prepared my boat for departure. Somehow, I had found the best rowing club on earth.

27

Disobedience

The woman who told me that transporting a boat was scary got it right. Every time I looked out the front window of my car, I saw the boat moving up and down. This would have been a source of consternation had not one of my friends anticipated this would happen and told me that the boat moving up and down was a good sign; moving sideways was bad.

After driving for two hours, I exited the highway and found the turn on to a dirt road leading to the lake. Its seeming interminability reminded me of the dirt road I had traveled to get to sculling school. This road ended in a parking lot below a rustic one-story building.

I parked far away from the other cars and walked toward the lake where I hoped to find the sandy beach with a swimming area that had been pictured on the website. It had looked like an ideal place to launch my scull. I thought I could carry my boat from the beach into shallow water and from there row on to the lake. But when I got to the swimming area, I saw that heavy ropes separated it from the lake. I knew that those ropes would snag my skeg, making it impossible for me to get out on the lake.

"Is there a dock for boats?" I asked a group of women from the workshop sitting on the beach. One of them pointed east.

The shoreline began to rise above the lake as I walked in the direction I had been sent. Within a hundred yards or so, I was looking down at the water from a rocky path. I saw a Sunfish tied up at a dock below, but the path leading there was steep and made treacherous by pine needle-covered tree roots. I didn't think I could walk down there safely by myself, let alone with a 26-foot-long boat.

Disheartened, I walked back to the swimming area. The women I had asked about a dock were still there and wanted to know if I had found a place to launch. When I told them why that dock wouldn't work, they mentioned that there was another one near the dining hall. I checked it out, but it was too high above the water to allow my rigger to rest flat on the dock to stabilize my boat. I couldn't even have gotten into the boat without capsizing with the rigger tilted at a twenty-degree angle.

I was hungry, exhausted, and overwhelmed. I had used supplies of reserve energy just to will the boat to stay on top of the car. My plan to launch from the swimming area had proven unworkable, as had alternatives. The rational thing to do was get in my car and drive home. But I knew I was too tired to make the drive back, so I decided to keep the boat on the car, check in, and figure out what to do in the morning.

I thought that getting a room would be a simple matter but the directions to my assigned cottage involved lots of indecipherable finger-pointing and hand-gesturing indicating "arounds" and "backs." One obstacle too many. My incipient meltdown must have been discernible because the woman handling registration offered to let me stay in the main building instead since it was a place I could at least find.

I liked my room despite its cot-sized bed, bare floor, and train-berth narrowness mostly because I had it to myself. I needed a cave at that point. And some moving meditation. Newton's First Law of Motion—a body at rest tends to stay at rest unless acted upon by some force—applies to my tendency to wallow in despondency unless I move. Doesn't matter where, doesn't matter how. It's as though being in motion rearranges my brain cells in a way that encourages information processing and decision-making.

Dinner was still hours away, so I decided to walk around. As I did, other women there for the workshop approached me to ask about my boat. I answered their questions and told them of the problems I had encountered finding a place to keep it. They assured me that there would always be someone at the swimming area to help me get over the ropes. I thought of all the people who had invested so much time and effort helping me get to Paradise Lake. I heard again their sincere wishes to have a good time. I could not break faith with them. And there was the matter of my dream of sculling on motorboat-free Paradise Lake. I took the boat out of the carrier, put it in slings I had set out at the periphery of the beach, and attached the riggers and foot stretcher while explaining what I was doing to a growing audience.

Dinner was an egg dish with cheese. I was hungry after I ate. I wanted to tell someone what I had gone through in the hope that that person would care and maybe try to convince me that everything would be okay, things would look better in the morning. But even if such a person had existed in my life, I wouldn't have been able to make a call because there was no cellphone service. Mercifully, I fell asleep as soon as I got into bed. It was the loons I heard the next morning that drew me to the open window. A perfect day for sculling.

I can get dressed to go out on the water while only partially awake. I used that automatic process because I feared that once my brain figured out what I intended to do, it would make me pack up, get in the car, and go home. I wasn't sure I wanted to do that with such a beautiful morning beckoning me to scull on Paradise Lake.

I waded into the swimming area with my boat on the top of my head. I wore flip-flops that were sucked into the sandy bottom as I walked, making every step an exercise in extraction and balance. When I was standing in about a foot and a half of water, I swung my boat off my head and onto the water. Then I secured oars in oarlocks, swung my legs over the hull one at a time, and scooted onto the seat. My entry was not a picture of grace, but I was in. I took a stroke and felt the movement I love: glide that synchronizes the rhythm of my heart with the movement of the boat.

To my amazement, I rowed over the swimming ropes and onto the lake without snagging my skeg. It was overcast and the wind had come up, but it didn't matter; I was on water I had only dreamed about, a lake off-limits to motorboats. I did not have to watch for waves caused by bass boats threatening to swamp my single. I did, however, have to watch for rocks and stayed in the middle of the lake while I explored. Surrounding mountains appeared to rise from the lake. I heard loons and then saw them. Their sound has been described as mournful, but to me it suggested a flute solo in a symphony of wind and water. I was happy. It started to rain. I didn't care. It rained harder. I didn't care.

I circumnavigated the lake and discovered that both outlets were impassable because of dense lily pad growth. I decided to go around one more time, but this time stayed to the leeward side of the lake to avoid waves starting to pick up as the wind increased. As I passed a rock sticking up from the water, with what I thought was a wide berth, I heard a sound that stopped my heart: crunching and scraping. I didn't know what I had hit and waited for the boat to split apart or for water to pour in through a hole in the bottom of the hull. When neither event occurred, I resumed breathing. I headed back; the rain hadn't let up and I didn't have a bailer. I turned so I could come in with my stern facing the beach and passed over the outer swimming rope. I wondered why I had been concerned about the ropes at all.

Then the second swimming rope snagged my skeg. I backed up and tried again. No movement off the rope. No one was around whom I could ask for help. I decided that the angle of the skeg was to blame, so I backed up and this time came in bow first. I passed over the outer rope with no problem but again caught on the second rope. As I sat, unable to move off the rope, two women came out of the dining hall, saw my predicament, and pressed down on the rope so that it was well under water and I could pass over it. I put the boat in slings and ran off to the dining hall for breakfast.

Poetic imagery, the first workshop that day, was held in a stone chapel surrounded by pines at the top of an overlook. I sat in a pew with windows open to the sound of birds and wrote lines of iambic pentameter, trying to capture the beating of my heart on the water that morning.

The second workshop, haiku, was a perfect summary of sculling. I wrote in my notebook, "it's the process that matters, there is no way to predict outcome." During a break, a woman in the workshop told me that she was journaling her prayers because she believed that prayer is nothing but worry asking for something we don't really want. It made sense to me that prayer and process were cousins with outcome a wild card

It was at lunch that day that I met the center's director, a nun who the other writers told me had single-handedly saved the lake from the auction block by making it self-supporting. Everything about her conveyed strength, from her no-nonsense, close-cropped hair to the way she sat in her chair, leaning on muscular arms ready to push away and raise her body for action. I should have walked by, but Miss Congeniality couldn't resist telling her how beautiful the lake was. Head nod. I went on about how ideal the lake was for rowing. A stare. I asked if she had thought about starting a weekend rowing program.

"I have but don't have the expertise." Terse.

"You could probably hire expertise without much difficulty."

"I don't have time." Dismissed.

The next morning, I took off in my scull as the retreat's care-taker ran back and forth on the beach shouting something at me that I was too far away to hear. It was another magical morning on glassy water. Varying how hard I drove off the foot stretcher,

I watched my puddles to judge how much intensity increased the distance between them. And then I stopped because I realized that I was making holes in the water, beautiful round circles with concentric rings. What I was doing was meaningless and beautiful, pure play. Blade poetry.

Déjà vu all over again for docking; I cleared the first rope but could not clear the second. As I was sitting there wondering if I had an energy bar stowed in my room to substitute for the breakfast I'd miss at the dining hall, a woman walked by, saw my predicament, and stomped on the rope. I broke free. My fellow writers were not only kind, but resourceful and smart. I had ten minutes before breakfast officially ended.

Just as I was putting some cantaloupe on my plate in the dining hall, the kitchen door swung open, and the director strode toward me. I thought she was coming over to tell me there was a one-piece limit on cantaloupe. I didn't know if a "cantaloupe rule" even existed, but I was ready to apologize anyway. I smiled in what I hoped was a disarming way.

She stood inches away from me as she shouted.

"You went out on the water without a lifejacket. There's a rule. No one goes out in a boat without a lifejacket. In fact, there's more than a rule—it's a state law, and you disobeyed."

Disobeyed. It had been so long since I had been charged with disobedience that I had forgotten whether it was a felony or a misdemeanor.

I started to tell her that I knew what the state law was, and federal law pre-empted it. She did not let me finish.

"I don't want to know what the law is. I am the law here, and you will not go out in your boat without a PFD," she said. If she had added "Little Missy," I would not have been surprised.

Much later, I understood that she wasn't talking about a life jacket. Here she was, in her mountain-lake fortress, like some noble warrior whose victory in retaining territory desired by the conquering forces had come at great personal cost, and I had come prancing in with my fancy boat no one had seen the likes of before, had attracted a lot of attention, and when she confronted me, I was not meek and accepting but stood my ground and used words like *pre-empted*, and in general acted like I knew more about sculling regulation than she did, which was true, except that I was on her turf, which turned out to be determinative. I decided that no approach would work with her, that no conciliatory tone or gesture would get me out on the water without wearing a bulky life jacket which, I knew, would jeopardize my safety by restricting movement. The only thing I knew to do was seek shelter. I left the following day.

28
Truth

I couldn't get to sleep the night before the club's annual fall regatta. Weeks before, my husband had announced that he wanted a divorce. I had lost my job and only been able to find part-time work, so listing my scant assets kept me awake at first, but then the knowledge I had been trying to hide from, that I was not loved, maybe never had been, slipped into bed, shrouding me with cold and making me afraid to sleep. Sometime after 4 a.m., I closed my eyes and fell into dreamless darkness. I woke to a 6 a.m. alarm. I wanted to find a dark cave, crawl in, curl into a fetal position and stay there forever, but I had promised I'd be at the boathouse at 7 a.m. to work the registration table. I knew I was counted on.

Everything seemed too bright when I arrived that early October morning. I must have registered people after I arrived, but I don't remember doing it. I only remember sitting slumped on the scratched brown metal chair behind the folding table and regretting that I hadn't brought sunglasses.

I was one of a team of three club members responsible for registering race entrants. One woman, a chemist, had memorized the order of the events for the day and the contents of the folders. When someone came to the table and told us the name of the race entered, she knew the precise location of that folder in the file box. I had to thumb through the folders until I got to the right one, sometimes going past it and thumbing through again. The other woman, a nuclear engineer, distributed the red and green shoelaces we were giving out as the club's regatta favor that year. She had batched the shoelaces into groups of nine and five so they were ready to be handed out to the eights and fours and their coxswains. I would have been counting them out one at a time, losing count, and then recounting while a line formed.

I was struck by how these women ordered their world, how they understood it in terms of numbers and arrangements of those numbers. Watching them go about their assigned tasks with efficiency and confidence, I thought about how I currently saw the world: not as categories that could be labeled and arranged, but as swirling chaos. They quantified; I entreated and hoped. They measured; I offered sacrifices to whatever gods might be disposed to dispense favors.

After registration ended, I watched scullers rigging shells, platoons of adolescents jogging down the dirt road parallel to the river, and dogs straining at leashes to get to other dogs. I smelled coffee and onions cooking. The sky was a reassuring blue. While I observed the festival, my chemist friend mentioned that there were no entrants in the open women's double event. I passively received the information.

"We could enter a boat and win," she said and then laughed.

At any other time in my life, I would have laughed too and let the moment pass. There was no invitation or suggestion in what she said; the humor was the contrast between fantasy and reality. But that day, I was a woman unmoored from her past, a woman who could risk because she had already lost.

"Okay, let's do it," I said.

She looked at me as though I had started speaking in tongues. "But we don't have a boat."

"We can get one," I said.

"How?"

"I'll ask if the club double is available, and if it's not, we'll row when it is."

"We're not registered."

"We're working registration; we'll just fill out a form and pay the fee."

"We've never rowed in a double together."

"We'll paddle down to the practice area and see what we can do," I said.

"I can't turn."

"I can."

"I want to row bow," she said.

"Fine with me."

"We don't know the course."

"The coxswain's meeting is in five minutes," I told her. "You go. I'll hold down your registration station."

I was on fire. I, who take three steps sideways and one step backward for every tentative step forward, obliterated every doubt, overcame every obstacle raised. Hacking through fear and self-doubt energized me. In fifteen minutes, we had a boat, mismatched oars, a bow number, advice about the turn, and a buzz going among the club members working the regatta. I wondered if this was how Cinderella must have felt before she entered the ballroom.

I had dressed for a day of sitting, not racing, so I ran to my car and rummaged through my duffel bag for lighter clothes that wouldn't restrict movement. I came up with an old pair of rowing shorts that had been in the bag all summer, part of my just-in-case-I-capsize wardrobe, and a turtleneck I knew would be too warm after we started racing. Still on world-record problem-solving pace, I rolled down the neck, pushed up the sleeves, and changed in the back seat of the car.

Our borrowed boat was a baby-blue Hudson about forty-five-feet long. We carried it out of the boathouse and queued behind other boats waiting for space on the dock. Standing there waiting, I had time to think. We had never sculled together and didn't know if we could. Some madness had brought me to this place where I was standing with a boat on my shoulder I had never rowed, listening for the call to advance to the dock, the music for our entrance. I could retreat to lucidity, go back to where I had been, but that made less sense than the crazy thing I was about to do.

Sitting in the boat at the dock, waiting for my partner to adjust her foot stretcher and tell me she was ready to push off, I resolved to not stick my hand in the river to take the water's temperature. I did not want to know how cold the water was. If we flipped the double, I wanted the temperature to be a surprise. Then she called "Ready," and we pushed off the dock. I was heartened immediately: we were two feet away from the dock and still sitting upright in the boat. She assumed bow duty and lined us up to cross the river for our trip downriver to the practice area.

The morning air was softening as it warmed in the autumn sun. A breeze moved the water as lightly as trailing fingers might. I felt some peace just being out on the water and for the moment did not care about the outcome of our race or even whether we stayed in the boat. Being part of the parade of boats paddling downriver was enough. The boat felt solid. We weren't rocking from side to side, and the wake from the stern didn't meander.

In the yes-we-can/no-we-can't negotiation that had gotten us out on the water, our fear that we would make fools of ourselves had been the last item on our agenda. We worried that it would take us so long to complete the course that our finish time, and we, would be a joke. We worried that boats scheduled to start well after we did would pass us while we were still on the course. We wanted to have fun, not be the object of it. To get past our fears, we redefined the race, agreeing that we would declare victory if we finished the three-mile course in under forty minutes without capsizing. We picked that number because it seemed a generous allotment of time. We had no idea how long it would take us to finish.

From working registration, we knew the racing order and sorted ourselves by asking other boats heading in the same direction which event they were entered in. When we identified a boat competing in the event after ours, my partner told them that the officials wanted them to start before us. They thanked us and rowed past. I wondered what had just happened. When they were several boat lengths away and out of earshot, I asked why she had told them they were supposed to go ahead of us.

"Because if they start ahead of us, they can't pass us on the course."

Her scientific mind had observed, deduced, and solved the problem of us being lapped.

Another women's double came up, and she hailed them. When they came alongside, she told them that they were to start ahead of us. Thanking her for the information, they disappeared upriver to the start. I kept a straight face and didn't lose a beat.

The official okayed us to go next. I gave the commands: "Half pressure," "Build to full pressure in two ... one, two," "Full pressure."

We were sculling with everything we had when we hit the orange plastic starting buoy. The race official on the riverbank above yelled at us to get off the buoy or we'd be disqualified. My partner called for a hard starboard stroke, but we the hit buoy again. The official continued to yell at us through his megaphone.

"You are interfering with the start. Move down now and restart, or you will be disqualified."

The orange plastic buoy was a veritable briar patch that did not want to let go of our trapped oars. Finally, we extricated ourselves, paddled a little downriver and managed to pass the buoy.

I settled into a rhythm: up the slide, quick catch, fast hands away, down the slide, repeat.

The boat felt good. Our catches were quiet but grabbed water. I heard the whir of seat wheels, the sound of oars turning and settling in the oarlocks, good boat music. My breathing even had a rhythm: quick and hard. I pushed against the foot stretcher and pulled the oars through the water, feeling the effort. We were moving the boat. We sculled in silence, concentrating, not wanting to use breath or energy for anything but the race. Even though I had no experience sculling with my new partner, I trusted her. Her objectivity, pragmatism, and adventurousness were all qualities I admired and had need of that day. As we approached our turnaround point, a friend of hers volunteering as a course marshal recognized her.

"Hey," he said from his launch. "Looking good. Keep going."

With about a mile left to go, I heard the sound of an engine before I saw the boat coming toward us. The race course was supposed to be closed to motorboat traffic, but that only meant that they traveled the river at the Coast Guard's discretion. Stopping motorboats for a few minutes to let shells and sculls through seemed to create a pent-up desire to make up for lost time. As this boat approached us, its wake created troughs deep enough for the double to start rolling. We stopped to wait out the wake's undulations.

We finished the course with no idea of our time. The boat had felt solid and faster than the forty minutes we had allowed for self-proclaimed victory, but we had no idea how much time we had used up at the start or waiting for the wake to subside. We were thrilled that we had stayed in the boat.

Race officials directed us toward the procession of boats headed for the practice area and the slow journey upriver ending in a long queue for dock space. But we didn't want to wait; we wanted to get out of our boat so we could ask someone at the timing table for our official elapsed time. As we crossed the river, an official came over in his launch to let us know we should follow the line of boats heading for the dock. My partner told him we were hot-seating our double and had to get back to the dock immediately. By now, I knew not to let my eyes widen or turn my head toward her and ask who needed the boat. She was so matter-of-fact in delivering the hot-seating fiction that there were two people waiting on the dock to hop into our boat as soon as we got out of it that I was swept along in the narrative's current and the adventure of the lie. I was an outlaw from my former life; everything seemed possible.

After we returned the double to its rack in the boathouse, we learned that our official time was 24:49. I thought I had heard wrong. The boat had felt good to me, but it didn't seem possible that after getting tangled up in the buoy and waiting for the wake to pass we had completed the course in record time. The only thing that stopped us from piling into our cars and presenting ourselves to the coaches at Olympic training camp as potential gold medalists was that we didn't know where the camp was.

When my female golden retriever was a year-and-a-half old, she became listless, almost neurasthenic. Home alone all day, it appeared the cure was another dog for company. Hindsight revealed that company was right, but dog wrong. Although I saw her as a dog, she saw herself as a cat and wanted feline company. The ten-week-old male golden retriever puppy who entered her life did give it purpose, however. Making his life a living hell animated her, put the gleam back in her eye, the prance in her step. She was such a sweet, gentle dog that I don't believe she was acting out of meanness. I think she sensed that there was limited time to convince him that she was to be feared and obeyed, and she was right. She seemed to shrink as he grew to twice her size. But even though he eventually grew taller and stronger, whenever he was in her presence, he believed he was a puppy whose stumpy legs were barely above grass level. Before the race, I had seen myself the same way in the presence of competition.

After the race, I felt like I had gone through a door I had been afraid to open. I had understood competition as somebody wins, somebody loses, someone is best, someone isn't good enough. It never entered my mind that competition could be redefined: stay in the boat, and you win. Have fun, and you win. I had taken a chance and, in doing so, changed my idea about what I could do. I didn't know what was ahead, but I believed that whatever it was, I'd find a way to get through it.

Epilogue

With my left hand on the dock, I push away, launching my scull toward the river, drifting until all twenty-six feet clear. I am underway, my voyage about to begin. I pull both oars through the water quietly, as though I am trespassing and don't want to be discovered. I feel my boat glide under me with sureness and purpose. Mid-river, I turn and head toward bridges, waterfalls, whatever I have designated as my destination in the scullers' sign-out book.

Once my bow is pointed in the direction I want to go, I focus on how the boat is moving. Am I settling into a rhythm that feels effortless, a cycle without beginning and end? Do I feel the boat ready to slip into a higher gear? I watch my hands and arms moving on their parallel path toward and away from bow and stern. I check behind me every ten strokes for other boats, logs, buoys. My breath syncs to the boat's movement. Up the slide, down the slide. I am coming alive.

I had sculled for a long time in frustration and fear. I sculled by concept, by words, trying to think a caress, to diagram love. Looking back, I wonder at my determination in persisting when I knew what I was doing wasn't working. Whether my perseverance when failure was the rule and progress all but indiscernible deserved reprimand or reward is difficult to know. Maybe I merited both. Head and heart argued:

You're lousy at this; you know you're lousy. Give it up.

I know I'm lousy at it, but I don't want to give it up. There's something about it that feels like falling in love.

There was truth in both perceptions. And uncharacteristically, I allowed myself to keep sculling despite my failure to achieve greatness immediately. Or ever.

I had been Skinny Minnie Fishtail, the Red Rover Queen of Yeadon, P.A., who could launch herself into a timeless world where she floated on a dream current. I had been a ballerina who loved the disciplined practice of grace, the possibility of poetry conferred by restriction of form. Both Red Rover and ballet had connected my mind, body, and soul. But connecting mind, body, and soul to my boat and river brought me to a different consciousness. After that, nothing felt as right as being in my scull.

Sculling is about becoming rhythm, the portal to glide. When I am moving no faster or slower than my boat, and my focus is intense enough to burn away errant thoughts, I imagine neurons in my brain moving like colored glass in a kaleidoscope. I hear the wheels of my seat moving along their metal tracks, oars turning in each oarlock, then entering the water—a bird's song, nothing more. Time slows, the rhythm of the boat moving through water carries me inside it like a wave curling toward shore. Body, boat, water, all vibrating to some cosmic tuning fork. I watch the puddles my oars make. Sometimes I see solar systems in the concentric circles; other times, the rings invite retrospection. Externally, nothing the least bit productive happens: I go up the river, I come down the river. But when I return to the dock, my entire being continues to hum.

I realize now that I had been searching for a long time for a way to return to that mind, body, soul alignment I had experienced as a child. I called it transformation but looked for it in all the wrong places, believing that only some kind of magic would restore what I had once known.

I had believed that transformation was the stuff of fairy godmothers: an incantation, and I'd be off to a life-changing ball in an exquisite gown. I discovered instead that the formula for transformation is *try, fail*, over and over, until one small thing changes. Repeat process. Transformation is not glamorous; there's no *abracadabra* instantaneous change. It's about endlessly coming up the slide, going back down the slide, paying attention to body, boat, water, connecting all three.

On summer mornings, I hear the river calling me: Red Rover, Red Rover... .

Acknowledgments

My heartfelt gratitude to all those who helped in the writing of this book. Special thanks and deep appreciation to Beth Petralia, my dear niece, for her unwavering encouragement and support. I also want to thank her for sending me a stuffed bear. He was a combination Maxwell Perkins and therapist.

I am profoundly grateful to Michael Sigman for believing in me, no matter what, and listening better than anyone on this earth.

Special thanks to Elizabeth Williams (starboard oar), for reading and championing my work and to Carol Carey and Nan Kuntz (port oars), for cheering me on. Their rowing excellence is surpassed only by their kindness.

I am grateful to Paul Lamar for reading my manuscript with loving attention and helping me see what was on the page.

Thank you to everyone in my writing group for honest feedback.

A deep bow to my editor, Michael Piekarski, who not only took on a newbie author but was unfailingly optimistic and patient as well. He should be sainted, not merely thanked.

Finally, my everlasting gratitude to my first editor, Le Anne Schreiber, who not only gave me permission to write about something I loved but helped me believe I could. *Requiescat in pace.*